CHARLIE PALMER'S
AMERICAN FARE

CHARLIE PALMER'S
AMERICAN FARE

Everyday Recipes from My Kitchens to Yours

Charlie Palmer

PHOTOGRAPHS BY ROBYN LEHR

GRAND CENTRAL
Life & Style
NEW YORK • BOSTON

Grand Central Life & Style

Hachette Book Group

1290 Avenue of the Americas

New York, NY 10104

www.GrandCentralLifeandStyle.com

Printed in the United States of America

WOR

First Edition: April 2015

10 9 8 7 6 5 4 3 2 1

Grand Central Life & Style is an imprint of Grand Central Publishing. The Grand Central Life & Style name and logo are trademarks of Hachette Book Group, Inc.

The Hachette Speakers Bureau provides a wide range of authors for speaking events. To find out more, go to www.HachetteSpeakersBureau.com or call (866) 376-6591.

The publisher is not responsible for websites (or their content) that are not owned by the publisher.

Library of Congress Cataloging-in-Publication Data

Palmer, Charlie, 1959-
   Charlie Palmer's American fare : everyday recipes from my kitchens to yours / Charlie Palmer. — First edition.
      pages cm
   Includes index.
   ISBN 978-1-4555-3099-1 (hardback) — ISBN 978-1-4555-3100-4 (ebook)
1. Cooking, American. I. Title. II. Title: American fare.
   TX715.P1637 2015
   641.5973—dc23
                        2014048819

Design by Gary Tooth / Empire Design Studio

To Courtland, Randall, Eric, and Reed: Everything always tastes better when we are eating it together. You are my greatest achievements.

....

To Lisa: Thank you, my love, for sharing dinners, glasses of wine, and your life with me, our four boys, and our dreams.

....

To my CPG team: You inspire me daily.

CONTENTS

CHARLIE PALMER'S
AMERICAN FARE

PROGRESSIVE AMERICAN COOKING:
IN THE RESTAURANT KITCHEN AND AT HOME

IT SHOULD COME AS no surprise that cooking is a rewarding profession. Seeing people's satisfaction as they put fork to mouth has remained one of the most sincere joys I've experienced in my thirty-five-year career and throughout my life. But I've come to realize two very important things about cooking: First is that the time I have spent cooking for my family has been the most rewarding. I'm incredibly fortunate to have four sons and my wife, Lisa, all of whom appreciate food and sharing time together around the table. Second, I take a huge amount of pride in teaching the young cooks and culinary students in my restaurant kitchens. Things have come full circle for me in that respect. I graduated from the Culinary Institute of America in 1979 and am now currently the chairman of the board of trustees of that school, helping to improve the quality of the education we provide to those young cooks every day.

When I began my culinary adventure in 1974, I had no idea of the magnitude of cuisines and products that would come to play in the invention of "new" American cooking or how they would impact the everyday American diet. Of course, I didn't know that I would become the father of four boys or have the opportunity to live in New York City, the most exciting city in the world, as well as Sonoma County, California, one of the most beautiful and agriculturally productive areas of the country. It is the combination of all these things that has broadened my own understanding of the evolution of cooking in America and the importance of the American family table.

I feel pretty lucky to continue to be inspired both by the diverse team of young chefs who work in my restaurants and by the inquiring minds of my sons. My own creativity is sparked by the integrity, intensity, and joy of their young palates. They are often the ones who lead me to new products, new growers, new flavors, new textures, and to dishes I would never have had the opportunity to taste. There is nothing more exhilarating than getting back on the line with the young guys in one of my restaurants or watching my sons devise a dish of their own without asking my advice.

So much has changed—in such a short time—in the way America eats. When I opened Aureole in 1988 just after the country's financial meltdown known as Black Monday, everyone thought I was crazy. But I felt that diners were ready to eat in a different way, experiencing flavors and textures with a mind open to adventure. I was right, but I had no idea where this audacious venture would take us. Flash-forward twenty-five years, and things are still rapidly changing both on the menu and at the bar. Serious beverage programs now include craft cocktails and beers and wide-ranging wine lists that offer bottles from the smallest producers to the more mainstream winemakers.

Fine dining is a way of life now that didn't seem possible only a few years ago. More people eat out nightly than ever before. Restaurant clientele is varied and smart. The food shows on television have made for a very informed dining public. Dress has become more casual and manners relaxed. More wine is served and interesting cocktails have to be on the menu. In our

restaurants we continue to push boundaries, serving innovative, creative, and delicious food and offering the refined service that knowledgeable diners expect.

When I came out of culinary school in 1979, nobody was talking about farm to table, environmentally sound agricultural practices, or sustainability in the kitchen. Growing up in upstate New York I knew that many people lived off the land, but I'd never put that lifestyle together with fine dining. However, I found myself in the first wave of American chefs who wanted to break barriers by embracing those ingredients native to the United States and traditional recipes that had often been overlooked, as French cuisine had a strong hold on fine dining. I quickly discovered that local and sustainable was part and parcel of this new outlook.

After I graduated from the Culinary Institute of America, I worked for the famed French chef Jean-Jacques Rachou at his acclaimed restaurant in New York City and then went on to work with the esteemed chef/restaurateur Georges Blanc in France. It was Rachou's demand for fresh, quality ingredients, as well as my experiences at Georges Blanc, where farmers and local culinary artisans would daily present their wares at the back door of the kitchen for the chef's approval, that awoke in me the possibilities of using the agricultural bounty of the United States in innovative American recipes. It radically changed my perspective to know that American cooking could easily transform itself into American "cuisine." That perspective has stuck with me over the years as I've opened restaurants

and hotels throughout the U.S., always looking toward the future and how I could do things better and more progressively in my kitchens, dining rooms, and, later, as a parent.

I spent a great deal of time formulating ideas of how I, as a trained chef, could use the experiences I had accumulated to help transform American dining. Once I manned my own kitchen, as chef-owner of Aureole, my first step was to research small, local, dedicated producers whom I could support by featuring their products on the Aureole menu. It was then that my style of cooking (which I eventually termed Progressive American) developed: using local, artisanal products and small farm producers to reinterpret classic European cooking for the American table.

In recent years I have found that almost every city, town, and village has a local farmers market, and farm stands dot roadsides all across America as well. These are the places where locals and weekenders gather, and from which their meals are often created. Often they

are a great locale for meaningful communication, the one spot where gossip is passed with impunity. Building relationships with farmers and producers can be done almost anywhere in the country; this makes the food you eat an even more personal experience. Throughout this book I will share some of the purveyors that I use, but I urge you to get to know all of the hardworking farmers and craftspeople in your area. The markets I visit now all have some of the essence of the old Les Halles: spectacular produce, freshly caught seafood, farm-raised game, innovative cheeses, breads even more seductive than those Parisian loaves of my early years, and, of course, their fair share of local characters.

From thinking locally, it has not been a far leap for me to begin to look at how products are being brought to market and how I could establish practices in the kitchen that would keep the environment safe for my family. And if you have children, you know how aware of the environment they are. In California, waste and water are far more regulated than they are in New York City, but I still try to follow some basic rules in my restaurants and at home in both areas.

Although locally sourced products continue to be a focus, there are many other aspects to address as we try to live a sustainable culinary life, one that ensures that we will have something valuable to pass on to our children and grandchildren.

The following will help establish a sustainable kitchen:

» Source local, organic ingredients in their season.

» Use everything you can in multiple ways.

» Use every part of herbs and vegetables.

» Use nontoxic cleaning products.

» Compost if you can; even in New York City, you can bring your compost to the farmers market.

» Recycle—both those items required by law and those that can be reused.

» Use biodegradable plastic and paper products.

» Grow your own when possible—even a city windowsill can make an herb garden.

» Conserve water as much as you can.

At home, each of my four guys looks at food and the environment in a different way; Courtland, now well into his university years and cooking for himself and others, sees the larger picture—food, wine, conversation—as a way to establish his own culinary identity with friends; Randall, son number two, is simply interested in eating and enjoying those foods he wants to eat; Eric and Reed, the twins and the youngest, are struggling with the idea that they might want to be in the business of food. They are the quickest to ask, "How did you learn about food?" Or, "Did your mom cook like you and did she teach you how to cook?" They want to know why and how I went to the Culinary Institute of America and what it meant to me. It's easy to see how much they miss their older brothers around the table and wait anxiously for the college breaks that bring them back home. To the twins, Sunday dinners just aren't the same without their bros.

My wife, Lisa, and I, like many parents, are not always home every night to cook. Cooking and managing my restaurants takes me all over the world and my daily work demands full attention to kitchens all across the country, but since the birth of my first son I have always managed to get home, if only for a few minutes, on most evenings; and no matter the challenge, weekends will find me in my own home kitchen. It is interesting that my boys think of me cooking for them nightly, and I think this is because the comfort of sitting together at the end of the day enjoying conversation and good food overshadows those missed nights.

So how does a family meal progress? Before doing any planning, I start by asking everyone what they feel like eating and then putting together what Courtland calls a drop-down meal. We decide on the protein—and with boys it has usually been a meat—which will be the foundation of the dinner. Then I work out the starch, vegetable, and salad. I don't on a daily basis add a dessert; that I save for weekends or special occasions, unless it's our family staple, Oatmeal Cookies (page 200).

Among the favorite main dishes at home are Mustard-Crusted Rack of Lamb (page 191); Crispy Lemon Chicken Cutlets (page 180); and my Grilled Tri-Tip Steak (page 185), all main courses that can also be found in a restaurant setting. At home and in my restaurants, I generally choose vegetables based on their season, which will send me out to a local farm in Sonoma or to the farmers market in New York City. Starch can be sticky rice, roasted potatoes (one of my favorites), a light pasta, or the boys' most-requested Double-Stuffed Potatoes (page 199). I always try to have a salad: coleslaw, butter lettuce with a lemon

vinaigrette, or whatever lettuce might be just popping up in the garden. Throughout the years, rather than always sticking to the traditional, I have tried to introduce new flavors and ethnic twists into our at-home meals as a way of bringing other cultures and flavors to the table, much as I continue to do in my restaurants.

I am often asked—by my sons and by young chefs and customers—how I come up with new recipes. I generally answer, "I've been at this for a long time, so over the years I've learned what tastes good and what ingredients complement each other." But even the most educated palate needs constant exposure to a broad intersection of the culinary world. For me that means everything from diner breakfasts to sushi to ramen to taco trucks to four-star dining at restaurants all across the world. This doesn't mean that I will copy a dish that I've experienced, but I will use my own palate to combine these new flavors or presentations with those from my past to create something that I hope will be totally new, yet still delicious. And sometimes an accident happens where flavors or combinations I am experimenting with meet

head-on; fireworks occur and a wonderful dish I hadn't imagined is born.

Wine is as much a part of our family table as it is in my restaurant dining rooms. The grapes for my Charlie Clay Russian River Pinot Noir grow right in my front yard in Sonoma. I host an annual event, Pigs & Pinot, where pork and pinot lovers from around the world gather at my hotel and restaurant, Hotel Healdsburg and Dry Creek Kitchen, to raise money for charity. Along with my Charlie Clay wine, I have two wines created exclusively for my restaurants and wine shop, Next Vintage: Iron Horse Aureole Cuvée, Green Valley; and Limestone Sauvignon Blanc, Dry Creek Valley. My son Courtland says, "As we have grown up, wine has more and more become essential to a family dinner, and more specifically to the hours leading up to it. Wine has become interesting to all of us, as we are able to differentiate varieties and flavors. We have been encouraged to taste wine for its flavor, not for its alcohol; we therefore see it as an exciting complement to our meals." I find this same sentiment true for our diners all across the country.

For my family, all of this is a continuum of our family table, and I am extremely proud that Lisa and I have prepared the boys for this new culinary world. Even now as they enter their late teens and early twenties, we continue to find time for as many dinners together as possible. Perhaps this is because I can then relax around the table with Lisa and the boys and get to know them in a very different way than when we watch them play sports, or achieve at school, or make new friends as we travel. Whether at home or in a restaurant setting, preparing great food and sharing delicious wine allows each of us to express ourselves in a very personal way. I believe that it is the shared table that has helped shape them into who they are today. The restaurant table is simply an extension of this shared experience as I continue to welcome diners to our tables all over the country. Whether cooking for your family or in a restaurant, I hope that in my recipe collection of American fare you will find dishes that you will want to make your own. This is how new and progressive cooking evolves.

Charlie Palmer
Spring, 2015

CHAPTER 1

SOUPS AND SALADS

On restaurant menus soups and salads are offered as a first course, but at home they stand alone. Almost all of these could be considered a full meal with a little bit of variation here and there. There are so many variations that it has been difficult to choose just a few that we enjoy around the family table. Both soups and salads offer ample opportunity to use leftovers and explore your own creativity. Don't like a particular green? Use a green you do like. For instance, as popular as kale currently is, I don't care for it raw and would never put it in a salad, but I like it cooked and in soups. If shrimp is not a favorite, try crab. Well, you get the idea—improvisation is the key to great soups and salads.

CHARLIE'S **CORN CHOWDER** WITH SHRIMP

Serves 6

10 ears corn, shucked

6 cups whole milk

2 cups chicken stock or canned nonfat, low-sodium chicken broth

¾ pound slab bacon, diced

1 cup chopped well washed leeks (white and some of the light green part)

½ cup diced red bell pepper

3 Yukon gold potatoes, peeled and cut into small dice

Salt and pepper

2 tablespoons chopped fresh chives, flat-leaf parsley, or cilantro

6 jumbo or 12 large cooked shrimp with tails on (see Note)

Cooking corncobs in milk and stock infuses this chowder with an intense corn flavor, a no-longer-secret technique that originally made this soup a namesake. If you would like to add a little heat to the soup, add some chopped chile pepper and garlic along with the leeks and bell pepper. The shrimp is not necessary, but it adds some heft and some sophistication to what is normally a home-style soup. Leftover soup can be pureed and served chilled with a swirl of heavy cream or yogurt.

Using a chef's knife and working with one at a time, cut close to each ear of corn to slice all of the kernels from the cob. Place the kernels in a mixing bowl and set aside. Reserve the cobs.

Combine the milk and stock in a large stockpot over medium-high heat. Add the cobs and bring to a boil. Lower the heat and simmer for about 15 minutes or until the liquid is infused with corn flavor.

Remove the pot from the heat and, using tongs, remove the cobs and set them aside until cool enough to handle. Do not discard the broth.

When the cobs are cooled, working with one at a time and holding the cob upright in a large shallow dish, carefully scrape all of the residue from them with the edge of a knife. Discard the cobs and add the scrapings to the broth.

Fry the bacon in a large frying pan over medium-low heat, stirring frequently, for about 15 minutes or until all of the fat has rendered out and the bacon is crisp. Using a slotted spoon, transfer the bacon to a double layer of paper towels to drain.

Pour off most of the fat from the frying pan, leaving about 1 tablespoon. Return the pan to medium heat and, when hot, add the leeks and bell pepper. Fry, stirring frequently, for about 7 minutes or until the vegetables have softened. Using a slotted spoon, transfer the vegetables to a double layer of paper towels to drain.

When the vegetables are well-drained of fat, transfer them to the broth. Place the pot over medium heat and bring to a simmer. Add the potatoes and season with salt and pepper. Bring to a boil.

Continued

Lower the heat and simmer for about 15 minutes or until the potatoes are tender.

Add the reserved corn kernels and again bring to a simmer. Simmer for about 6 minutes or just until the corn is barely cooked.

Remove about 2 cups of the chowder from the pot and place in a blender or food processor fitted with the metal blade. Process to a thick puree. Pour the puree back into the chowder and simmer for another 5 minutes.

Remove the chowder from the heat and stir in the reserved bacon along with the herb of choice. Taste and, if necessary, adjust the seasoning with salt and pepper.

Serve piping hot in large shallow soup bowls with 1 jumbo shrimp or 2 large shrimp in the center of each bowl.

Note: You can also add an additional ¾ pound chopped raw shrimp to the soup after you have pureed the 2 cups. The 5-minute reheat will cook the shrimp perfectly.

THE BEST **POTATO** SOUP

Serves 6

½ pound slab bacon, diced

3 tablespoons unsalted butter

6 leeks (white part only),
well washed and sliced crosswise
into chunks

2½ pounds all-purpose potatoes,
peeled and cubed

5 cups chicken stock or canned
nonfat, low-sodium chicken broth

3 cups half-and-half

Salt and pepper

1 cup heavy cream

2 tablespoons chopped fresh dill or
flat-leaf parsley

The combination of potatoes, leeks, and bacon has always been at the top of my flavor chart—both growing up in upstate New York and as a chef trained in the French style. My mom called it "warm-up potato soup," which is exactly what it did on a cold, snowy winter's day. As a young chef in France I learned about vichyssoise, a more refined version of my mom's warm-up that can also be served chilled. Either way—hot or cold—potatoes and leeks combined with a hint of smoky bacon is, to me, a terrifically satisfying dish.

Fry the bacon in a frying pan over low heat, stirring frequently, for about 15 minutes or until the fat has rendered out and the bacon is brown and crisp. Using a slotted spoon, transfer the bacon to a double layer of paper towels to drain.

Place the butter in a large saucepan over medium heat. When melted, add the leeks and cook, stirring frequently, for about 8 minutes or until the leeks are very soft and fragrant but have not colored.

Add the potatoes along with the stock and half-and-half and bring to a boil. Season with salt and pepper, remembering that the bacon will add a bit of saltiness. Lower the heat and cook at a gentle simmer for about 18 minutes or until the potatoes are about to fall apart. At this point you can, if you wish, puree the mix in a blender or food processor for a smoother, creamier soup.

Whether left chunky or pureed, add the cream and cook for an additional 10 minutes. Taste and, if necessary, season with additional salt and pepper.

Remove from the heat and stir in the reserved bacon along with the dill. Serve immediately in large shallow soup bowls.

SUMMER MINESTRONE
WITH MINT PESTO

Serves 6

3 large (about 1 pound) very ripe tomatoes, peeled, cored, seeded, and cut into pieces

10 cups vegetable stock or canned, nonfat, low-sodium vegetable broth

1½ cups fresh cranberry beans

1 cup finely diced carrots

½ cup finely diced Vidalia or other sweet onion

Salt and pepper

¾ cup finely diced yellow squash

¾ cup finely diced zucchini

¾ cup fresh English peas

¾ cup fresh corn kernels

1 teaspoon lemon juice

Mint Pesto (recipe follows), optional

Having grown up in upstate New York, where there are long winters and a short growing season, I still am amazed at the year-round bounty of California farmers. So although this soup has summer in its title, I can now make it almost all year long in Sonoma, while folks in the East have to wait for warmer weather. While a winter minestrone is a heavy soup with root vegetables and pasta, this is a *minestrina*, a thin soup with a light broth and barely cooked vegetables that say local and sustainable in a bowl. The pesto is not absolutely necessary, but it does add a whole new dimension to the soup.

Place the tomatoes in the bowl of a food processor fitted with the metal blade and process to a smooth puree.

Combine the tomato puree with the vegetable broth in a large saucepan over medium heat. Add the beans, carrots, and onion. Season with salt and pepper and bring to a simmer. Simmer for 10 minutes or just until the beans begin to soften. Stir in the yellow squash, zucchini, peas, and corn and again bring to a simmer. Simmer for about 12 additional minutes or until the vegetables have softened slightly but remain a bit crisp. Add the lemon juice, taste, and, if necessary, season with additional salt and pepper.

Remove from the heat and ladle into large shallow soup bowls. If using, spoon a dollop of pesto into the center and serve.

MINT PESTO

Makes about 1½ cups

2 cups loosely packed mint leaves

3 cloves garlic, chopped

½ cup chopped toasted hazelnuts

½ cup freshly grated Parmesan cheese

½ to ¾ cup extra-virgin olive oil

Salt and pepper

Combine the mint with the garlic, nuts, and cheese in the bowl of a food processor fitted with the metal blade and process just until the mixture is thick and paste-like. With the motor running, slowly add enough of the oil to make a textured, but not chunky, thick sauce. Season with salt and pepper.

Use immediately or store, tightly covered and refrigerated, for up to 3 days.

Note: If you want to make a traditional Italian basil-based pesto, replace the mint with fresh basil leaves and the hazelnuts with toasted pine nuts.

RED ONION SOUP

Serves 6

¼ cup (½ stick) unsalted butter

5 medium red onions (about 1½ pounds), thinly sliced

3 leeks (white and some of the light green part), well washed and cut crosswise into thin slices

1 cup thinly sliced shallots

1 teaspoon minced garlic

2 tablespoons balsamic vinegar

1 teaspoon fresh thyme leaves

1 cup dry red wine

5 cups chicken stock or canned nonfat, low-sodium chicken broth

4 cups beef stock or canned nonfat, low-sodium beef broth

Salt and pepper

6 large slices toasted baguette

½ cup grated Gruyère cheese

This isn't exactly the same soup as the one I learned to love in Paris so many years ago. But it is, perhaps, even better. Red onions add a depth of sweetness that onion soups made with white onions lack. This is my go-to soup during football season, particularly when I'm in New York rooting for my favorite team, the New York Giants. I've even packed it into a thermos—without the bubbling cheese—and carried it to the stadium to warm my boys and me when we're freezing our butts off in the stands.

Heat the butter in a large heavy-bottomed soup pot over medium heat. Add the onions, leeks, shallots, and garlic and cook, stirring occasionally, for about 12 minutes or just until the mixture begins to color. Immediately adjust the heat to the lowest possible setting and continue to cook, stirring occasionally, for about 30 minutes or until the onion mixture is richly colored, almost a deep brown. Throughout the cooking process, watch very carefully as you do not want the butter to burn. If this begins to happen, add another tablespoon of butter along with a tablespoon or two of water.

Stir in the vinegar and thyme and cook for a couple of minutes. Add the red wine, raise the heat, and bring to a simmer. Simmer for about 10 minutes or until some of the wine has cooked off. Stir in the chicken and beef stocks and season with salt and pepper. Bring to a simmer and then lower the heat. Cook for about 20 minutes or until the soup has developed a rich brown color and is very aromatic.

Just before the soup is ready, preheat the broiler.

When ready, ladle the soup into crocks or deep heat-proof bowls. Place the toasts on top of the soup in each crock and sprinkle the cheese over all.

Place under the broiler for about 2 minutes or until the cheese is bubbling and golden brown.

Remove from the broiler and serve immediately, giving everyone a warning to be extra careful of the hot crocks and the extremely hot cheese.

HEARTY KALE SOUP

Serves 6 to 8

1 pound kale, tough stems removed

1 pound lean smoky bacon, diced

2 cups diced onions

1 tablespoon minced garlic

8 cups chicken stock or canned
nonfat, low-sodium chicken broth

1 pound red potatoes, unpeeled
and diced

3 cups cooked white (small white,
cannellini, or navy) beans

Salt and pepper

Red pepper flakes

This soup is based on a classic Portuguese kale soup made with linguiça, a traditional smoked sausage. It has been made in home kitchens for years—long before the current rage for all things kale. My version keeps the kale, but replaces the sausage with bacon and adds beans for an even heartier mix. This is a terrific winter soup that is filling enough to be dinner with lots of crusty bread, a big salad, and, of course, a glass or two of pinot.

Working with about 5 leaves at a time, neatly stack the kale and then roll the stack into a tight cigar shape. Using a sharp knife, cut the roll crosswise into thin slices. Unroll and pull apart into strips. Continue cutting until all of the kale is in strips. Set aside.

Fry the bacon in a large frying pan over medium heat, stirring frequently, for about 12 minutes or until all of the fat has been rendered out and the bacon is very crisp. Using a slotted spoon, transfer the bacon to a double layer of paper towels to drain.

Keeping the pan on medium heat, add the onions and garlic to the bacon fat and sauté for about 6 minutes or until just beginning to sweat their liquid. Scrape into a soup pot.

Add the chicken stock to the soup pot along with the potatoes, beans, and reserved kale. Season with salt, pepper, and red pepper flakes and place over medium-high heat. Bring to a boil, stirring occasionally to evenly distribute the kale. Once boiling, immediately lower the heat to a gentle simmer. Simmer for about 30 minutes or until the potatoes are cooked and the soup is very flavorful.

Remove from the heat, stir in the reserved bacon, and serve with lots of crusty bread for dunking.

NEXT DAY
CHICKEN SOUP

Serves 6

10 cups chicken stock (see Note)

4 ounces basmati or jasmine rice

1½ cups finely diced carrots

1½ cups finely diced celery

1½ cups frozen petit peas, thawed

Salt and pepper

1 tablespoon finely chopped fresh
flat-leaf parsley or dill

My four sons sipped plenty of this soup throughout the years. As any parent knows, once one child catches something, the others seem to also! I think it has been proven medically that chicken soup heals, but I can guarantee that it does as I've watched it revive the boys over and over again. Although many chicken soups are made by creating a broth using a whole chicken (see Note), I always have a rich, homemade chicken stock on hand, which is especially nourishing. You can certainly add chunks of cooked chicken to the soup just before serving if that pleases you, and it always tastes just as good, if not better, the next day.

Bring the stock to a simmer in a soup pot over medium heat and add the rice. Return to a simmer and cook for about 12 minutes or just until the rice is beginning to soften. Stir in the carrots and celery and again return to a simmer. Simmer for about 6 minutes or until the rice is tender. Add the peas; taste and, if necessary, add salt and pepper. Simmer for an additional 2 minutes or just until the peas are hot.

Remove from the heat, stir in the chopped parsley, and serve.

Notes: If you want to base the soup on a whole chicken cooked to make the broth, by all means do so. Place a whole chicken in a large soup pot along with a chopped carrot, onion, and celery rib. Add some peppercorns, salt, and herbs if you wish. Cover with a good amount of water (it should cover the chicken by about 2 inches) and bring to a boil. Reduce the heat and simmer, skimming off the fat that rises to the top, for about 1 hour, or until the chicken is pulling away from the bone and the broth is very flavorful. Lift the chicken from the pot and set aside until cool enough to handle. Strain and return the broth to the pot. Add the vegetables from the basic recipe and cook as directed. While the soup is cooking, pull the meat from the bones and add it to the pot just before the soup is ready.

You can also use chicken parts to make a stock in this same manner and, if you like, roast the parts before simmering for a darker, richer broth. Canned broth with some chicken wings added for fresh flavor can also do the trick.

For a nontraditional touch, you can add a few slices of fresh ginger to the pot of soup, particularly during flu season, as folk and Chinese medicines recommend ginger for its healing properties.

YELLOW EYE AND CHORIZO SOUP

Serves 6 to 8

---

1 pound yellow eye beans, rinsed

6 cloves garlic, peeled

4 sprigs fresh thyme

1 onion, chopped

Zest of 1 organic orange (removed with a vegetable peeler)

Salt and pepper

¼ cup olive oil

½ pound Spanish chorizo (see Note), cut into small pieces

3 tablespoons chopped fresh flat-leaf parsley

1 teaspoon hot paprika

Although I'm partial to California's Sonoma County, Napa does have one thing we don't—Rancho Gordo, a purveyor of heirloom dried beans and seeds (see Sources, page 243). They offer a variety not seen otherwise, and most of them are grown locally. Yellow eye beans are one of my favorites as they are extremely dense and creamy and create a rich, velvety soup. If you can't find them, you can use navy or cannellini beans as a substitute.

Place the beans in a large soup pot with cold water to cover and set aside to soak for at least 6 hours or as long as overnight.

Drain well and return the beans to the pot. Add cold water to cover by at least 2 inches and place over high heat. Bring to a boil and add the garlic, thyme, onion, and orange zest. Lower the heat and cook at a gentle simmer for about 1 hour. Season with salt and pepper and continue to simmer for another 30 minutes or until the beans are very tender. If necessary, add water to keep the broth very liquid.

While the beans are cooking, prepare the chorizo.

Heat the olive oil in a large frying pan over medium heat. Add the chorizo and fry, stirring frequently, for about 12 minutes or until almost crisp. Using a slotted spoon, transfer the chorizo to a double layer of paper towels to drain. Reserve the oil.

Remove and discard the thyme sprigs from the beans. Transfer the cooked beans to a blender and process to a smooth puree. This will probably have to be done in batches. If the finished puree is too thick, add either water or chicken stock to thin to a soup consistency.

Transfer the puree to a large clean saucepan. Stir in the parsley and paprika along with the reserved chorizo and bring to a simmer. Taste and, if necessary, add salt and pepper.

Ladle the soup into large shallow bowls, drizzle the reserved chorizo cooking oil over the tops, and serve.

Note: In California, we have a terrific store in Mill Valley, The Spanish Table, that features superb Spanish food products (including chorizo) and kitchen items. In New York, Despaña Foods of Spain supplies home cooks and chefs alike with premier Spanish products. If you don't have such wonderful stores nearby, La Tienda (see Sources, page 243) is the go-to online source.

CHOPPED SALAD

Serves 6

1 Hass avocado, peeled and cut into chunks

1 tablespoon very finely chopped shallot

1 teaspoon Dijon mustard

3 tablespoons champagne vinegar

¼ cup extra-virgin olive oil

4 ounces Point Reyes blue cheese, crumbled

Salt and pepper

2 romaine hearts, chopped

3 cups chopped iceberg lettuce

2 Kirby cucumbers, seeded and chopped

1 small head radicchio, trimmed and chopped

1 small fennel bulb, trimmed, cored, and chopped

1 carrot, peeled and finely chopped

2 tablespoons chopped fresh chives

Chopped salads seem to be more popular on the East Coast than on the West, particularly for ladies meeting for a business lunch. They can be as simple as a couple of types of lettuces chopped together and lightly dressed or as complex as a mix of chopped vegetables and meats. This is a relatively easy one made extraordinary with a blue cheese dressing made with blue cheese from the award-winning Point Reyes Farmstead Cheese Company, a local Sonoma favorite (see Sources, page 243).

Place the avocado in a shallow bowl and, using a kitchen fork, mash until smooth. Add the shallot and mustard and stir to blend. Whisk in the vinegar and, when blended, whisk in the oil. Add half of the blue cheese and whisk until creamy. Season with salt and pepper.

Combine the romaine and iceberg lettuces in a large bowl. Using your hands, toss to mix. Then add the cucumbers, radicchio, fennel, carrot, and chives, tossing until thoroughly combined.

Drizzle the dressing over the salad and toss until all of the ingredients are lightly coated.

Transfer to a large salad bowl and sprinkle the remaining blue cheese over the top. Serve immediately.

Note: You can turn this into a restaurant-style salad by packing the dressed salad into lightly oiled 6-ounce soufflé dishes and then turning each upside down onto the center of a plate. Make extra dressing to drizzle around the edges of the plates and garnish the salads with the blue cheese along with herb sprigs, cherry tomatoes, and/or crumbled crisp bacon. You can also form the salad in a large ring mold.

THREE FAVORITE COLESLAWS

On a trip to the supermarket awhile back, I was surprised by the selection of packaged slaw mixes in the produce department. Like most home cooks, I am often only interested in getting food on the table as quickly as I can, particularly when I have a pack of hungry teenage boys at the door. So I bought a couple of those time-saving coleslaw mixes to experiment with and found that the end results pleased everybody. Here is a recipe that resembles my mom's original and two others that came out of that first try.

1

ALMOST MY MOM'S COLESLAW

Serves 6 to 8

1 (2-pound) firm head green cabbage

1 large carrot, peeled

1 cup Miracle Whip salad dressing

3 tablespoons white vinegar

1 tablespoon sweet pickle juice

1 teaspoon Dijon mustard

½ teaspoon celery seed

Salt and pepper

It took me awhile to figure out why all homemade traditional coleslaws never taste like the kind you get commercially, or like my mom's. And since that is the flavor most familiar to me, I determined to figure it out. Here's what I found: You have to use Miracle Whip salad dressing as the base, and you need just a hint of juice from sweet pickles to mellow it out.

Core and wash the cabbage. Drain very well and pat as dry as you can.

Shred the cabbage in a food processor fitted with the shredder blade, or by hand using a sharp chef's knife. Place the shredded cabbage in a large mixing bowl.

Grate the carrot in the same fashion or on the coarse side of a handheld grater and add to the cabbage. Toss to blend.

Combine the salad dressing, vinegar, pickle juice, mustard, and celery seed in a small bowl, whisking to blend thoroughly. Season with salt and pepper.

Pour the dressing over the cabbage mixture, tossing to coat evenly.

Serve immediately or store, covered and refrigerated, for up to 4 hours. Longer storage is fine, but the cabbage will wilt considerably.

SPICY CITRUS-SOY SLAW

Serves 6 to 8

1 (12-ounce) package prepared coleslaw mix (green and red cabbage with carrots)

1 bunch radishes, cleaned and thinly sliced

1 cup finely diced jicama

⅓ cup soy sauce

2 tablespoons orange juice

1 tablespoon rice wine vinegar

1 tablespoon honey or light brown sugar (or to taste)

⅓ cup sesame oil

1 tablespoon shichimi togarashi (see Note) or red chile flakes

2 teaspoons black or toasted sesame seeds

Salt

This is a tasty slaw that offsets the sweet with a kick of heat.

Combine the slaw mix with the radishes and jicama in a large mixing bowl. Set aside.

Combine the soy sauce, orange juice, rice wine vinegar, and honey in a small mixing bowl, whisking to blend. Whisk in the sesame oil. Add the shichimi togarashi and sesame seeds. Taste and, if necessary, season with salt and/or additional honey.

Drizzle the dressing over the cabbage mixture, tossing to coat.

Serve immediately or store, covered and refrigerated, for up to 4 hours. Longer storage is fine, but the cabbage will wilt considerably.

Note: Shichimi togarashi is an everyday Japanese spice mix of at least seven different seasonings: ground chile pepper, orange peel, black and white sesame seeds, ginger, sansho, nori, and hemp seeds. It adds a complex zest to dishes, even those that do not reflect Japanese cuisine. It is available from Asian markets, specialty food stores, and some supermarkets, or, of course, online. It is also known as 7-spice powder.

BROCCOLI SLAW

Serves 6 to 8

1 (12-ounce) package broccoli slaw

½ pound bacon, fried and crumbled

½ cup finely diced red onion

½ cup mayonnaise

½ cup sour cream

1 tablespoon lemon juice

1 tablespoon sugar

½ teaspoon poppy seeds

Salt and pepper

This slaw is a change from the usual, with even more crunch from using the unexpected vegetable, broccoli.

Combine the broccoli slaw mix with the bacon and red onion in a large bowl, tossing to blend.

Combine the mayonnaise, sour cream, lemon juice, sugar, and poppy seeds in a small bowl, whisking to blend. Pour the dressing over the broccoli mixture, tossing to coat. Taste and, if necessary, season with salt and pepper.

Serve immediately or store, covered and refrigerated, for up to 4 hours. If you do the latter, do not add the bacon until you are ready to serve.

A REAL CHEF'S SALAD

Serves 6 to 8

1 large head romaine lettuce, well-washed, dried, and roughly chopped

Thousand Island (or Russian) Dressing (recipe follows)

½ pound rare roast beef, julienned

½ pound prosciutto, rolled into cylinders

½ pound smoked chicken breast, julienned

¼ pound Vella (see Vella Cheese, pages 73, 243) or other artisanal cheddar cheese, cubed

¼ pound Gruyère cheese, cubed

12 heirloom cherry tomatoes, halved

1 large watermelon radish, thinly cut crosswise

1 sweet onion, thinly sliced crosswise

2 cups croutons

---

1 cup mayonnaise

¼ cup Heinz chili sauce (see Note)

1 hard-boiled egg, peeled and finely chopped

3 tablespoons sweet pickle relish

1 tablespoon lemon juice

1 teaspoon Worcestershire sauce

Salt and pepper

One of my first "important" chef jobs was at a very exclusive country club where the members counted on great meals in their clubhouse. I worked hard to fulfill the requirements, and one of the lunch requests was for a classic chef's salad. This recipe is just about the same as the one I made years and years ago, but the ingredients now reflect the extraordinary artisanal products always at hand. This is really just a composed salad in which you can use a combination of whatever meats, poultry, cheese, and garnishes you like as long as you arrange them in an inviting pattern on the plate.

Toss the lettuce with about ½ cup of the dressing in a large wooden salad bowl. (The lettuce should just be lightly coated with the dressing.) Place the roast beef in a circle around the edge of the salad bowl. Then make a circle of rolled prosciutto followed by a circle of smoked chicken. Place the two cheeses in the center of the ring of meats. Place a circle of tomato between the roast beef and prosciutto and the radish slices around the edge of the bowl. Pull the onion slices apart and place the rings over the top of the salad. Sprinkle croutons over the top and drizzle some of the remaining dressing over the top. Serve with the remaining dressing passed on the side.

THOUSAND ISLAND (OR RUSSIAN) DRESSING

Makes about 1½ cups

There seems to be an ongoing debate about what differentiates Thousand Island from Russian dressing. I use the terms interchangeably, but some cooks feel that Russian dressing is a bit tangier and should be made with herbs and pimentos, while Thousand Island should have chopped olives and vegetables. I'll stay out of the debate and just use my version.

Combine the mayonnaise with the chili sauce in a small mixing bowl. Stir in the egg, relish, lemon juice, and Worcestershire sauce. Taste and, if necessary, season with salt and pepper.

Serve or store, covered and refrigerated, for up to 1 week.

Note: Heinz chili sauce is what makes a true Thousand Island dressing. But if you are in a rush and don't have it on hand, use ketchup.

SLOW-ROASTED
BEET SALAD

Serves 6

Rock salt (see Note)

6 large beets, well-scrubbed and cut into 3- to 4-inch pieces

2 tablespoons olive oil

2 shallots, minced

¾ cup chopped toasted sunflower seeds

2 tablespoons chopped fresh flat-leaf parsley

Citrus Vinaigrette (recipe follows)

3 small bunches mâche lettuce

8 ounces creamy fresh goat cheese

Beets and goat cheese have been on my menu for years and years. I found that the combination will always turn beet haters into beet lovers. The citrus vinaigrette is also perfect for simple green salads using sweet lettuces, such as Bibb, mâche, or oak leaf.

Preheat the oven to 325°F.

Line a shallow baking dish (I use a 6-quart Staub cocotte or casserole) or rimmed baking sheet with a ½-inch layer of rock salt.

Rub the beets with olive oil and nestle them into the salt at least 1 inch apart. Roast for about 90 minutes or until the beets are tender when poked with the point of a small sharp knife. Using tongs, lift the beets from the salt. Set aside until cool enough to handle.

Using your fingertips, push the skins from the beets and discard. Cut the beets into 1½-inch chunks and place in a mixing bowl. Add the shallots, sunflower seeds, and parsley, tossing to blend. Drizzle with about ¼ cup of the vinaigrette, tossing to coat evenly.

Place a mound of mâche on each of 6 luncheon plates. Spoon an equal portion of the beet salad over the top. Garnish with a heaping spoonful of goat cheese and drizzle vinaigrette around the edge of the plates.

Note: If you don't have rock salt or can't find it, you can use an equal amount of coarse or kosher salt.

¼ cup white wine vinegar

2½ tablespoons lemon juice

2½ tablespoons orange juice

1 small shallot, minced

1 teaspoon finely chopped fresh
flat-leaf parsley

¾ cup extra-virgin olive oil

Sea salt and pepper

CITRUS VINAIGRETTE

Makes about 1½ cups

Combine the vinegar and lemon and orange juices in a small mixing bowl. Stir in the shallot and parsley. Whisking constantly, slowly add the oil. When emulsified, season with salt and pepper.

Serve immediately or place in a nonreactive container, cover, and store, refrigerated, for up to 3 days. Bring to room temperature before using.

WARM PORK AND **LENTIL SALAD**

Serves 6 to 8

1 (2-pound) pork tenderloin, trimmed of all fat and silverskin

1 teaspoon cayenne pepper (or to taste)

2 tablespoons lemon juice

2 tablespoons soy sauce

4 cups well-drained cooked red lentils (see Note)

¾ pound fresh goat cheese, crumbled

3 tablespoons chopped fresh flat-leaf parsley

2 tablespoons minced shallot

1 teaspoon minced fresh thyme

3 tablespoons peanut oil

1 teaspoon Dijon mustard

Salt and pepper

4 cups chicory, trimmed and chopped

Pork tenderloin is so easy to prepare. It is mildly flavored and very tender, cooks quickly, and works well with almost any seasoning and in any type of cuisine. What more could a cook want? Plus, I've never found anyone who didn't like it. The soy sauce and goat cheese add just the right amount of flavor to this interesting and healthy salad.

If you can't find red lentils, any other lentil or small bean would also work just fine.

Preheat the oven to 450°F.

Rub the tenderloin with the cayenne, coating all sides. Combine 1 tablespoon each of the lemon juice and soy sauce and rub over the cayenne-coated meat. Place on a rack in a roasting pan and roast for 12 minutes. Lower the temperature to 375°F and continue to roast for another 10 minutes or until an instant-read thermometer inserted into the thickest part of the tenderloin reads 140°F. (The meat will continue to cook once removed from the oven.) Let rest about 10 minutes or until an instant-read thermometer inserted into the thickest part reads 150°F.

Lower the oven temperature to 300°F.

While the meat is cooking, combine the lentils in a mixing bowl with ½ pound of the goat cheese, 1 tablespoon of the parsley, the shallot, and the thyme. Add the remaining 1 tablespoon each of the lemon juice and soy sauce. Whisk the oil and mustard together and pour over the lentil mixture, stirring to blend. Season with salt and pepper.

Place the chicory in an even layer on an ovenproof platter. Spoon the lentil mixture down the center of the chicory.

Using a sharp chef's knife, cut the pork crosswise on the bias and nestle the slices in the lentils. Sprinkle the salad with the remaining ¼ pound goat cheese and place in the oven for 5 minutes.

Remove from the oven, sprinkle the salad with the remaining 2 table-spoons parsley, and serve.

Note: Red lentils cook very quickly. They can turn to mush in seconds, so they have to be watched carefully. You want them to be just barely soft, but still holding their shape. This should take no longer than 12 minutes in boiling unsalted water.

SMOKED CHICKEN SPRING SALAD WITH RYE BERRIES AND SWEET PEAS

Serves 6

6 tablespoons extra-virgin olive oil

2½ tablespoons champagne vinegar

1 clove garlic, minced

1 teaspoon grated lemon zest

Salt and pepper

4 cups cooked rye berries (see Note)

2 cups chopped smoked chicken

1½ cups English peas
(about 1 pound in the shell),
barely steamed

1 cup diced fennel

3 teaspoons chopped fresh
chives, dill, or fennel fronds

8 to 10 leaves radicchio, optional

It has been remarkable to see the introduction of so many grains into our menus. Rice was about the only one I cooked with in my early days as a chef. Rye berries are unusual and quite potent in flavor. I find them intriguing and will engage diners in a contest to identify the taste. However, if you try them and don't like them, replace them with any other wheat berry or rice. This is a simple but very nourishing salad that reflects the current interest in healthy eating. If the flavors are too strong, don't hesitate to add some dried cranberries or cherries or even raisins to mellow the salad.

Combine the olive oil, vinegar, garlic, and lemon zest in a small bowl. Season with salt and pepper and whisk the dressing to blend thoroughly.

Combine the rye berries with the chicken, peas, fennel, and 2 teaspoons of the chives in a large bowl. Add the dressing and toss to blend completely.

Serve as is or line a serving platter with the radicchio and mound the salad in the center. Garnish with the remaining 1 teaspoon chives.

Note: To cook rye berries, first toast them in a dry frying pan for about 5 minutes or until they begin to color and are quite fragrant. Place in cold water to cover and soak for at least 1 hour or up to 12 hours; drain well. For every cup of rye berries, combine them with 2 cups salted water in a medium saucepan over medium-high heat. Bring to a boil, lower the heat to a simmer, and cook covered for about 1 hour or until very tender. One cup of rye berries will yield 3 cups cooked. As noted, don't hesitate to substitute any cooked grain, including brown or wild rice, for the rye berries.

SALMON SALAD
WITH SPINACH, PEA SHOOTS, AND ARTICHOKES

Serves 6

6 (5- to 6-ounce) center-cut skinless salmon fillets, pin bones removed

1 tablespoon grapeseed oil

Salt and pepper

8 cups baby spinach

4 cups fresh pea shoots

Black Olive Vinaigrette (recipe follows)

6 marinated artichoke hearts, cut into quarters

Before I was herding four boys around, I might have made the marinated artichoke hearts from scratch. But home cooking is different from restaurant cooking, and once I became a father I did learn to take shortcuts. As the boys leave home, I may well go back to cooking the artichokes from scratch, but for now I am perfectly happy with commercially packaged artichoke hearts. Sometimes you might want to add some herbs, heat, or acid, but they still save a ton of time and taste very good.

Lightly coat both sides of the salmon with the grapeseed oil. Season with salt and pepper.

Preheat a nonstick stovetop grill pan over high heat.

When very hot, add the salmon and grill, turning once, for about 6 minutes (for rare) to 8 minutes (for medium).

While the salmon is cooking, combine the spinach and pea shoots in a mixing bowl. Add just enough of the vinaigrette to lightly coat.

Place the greens on a serving platter. Place the salmon fillets among the greens. Sprinkle the artichoke quarters around the salmon on the platter, and drizzle some of the remaining vinaigrette over the tops and around the edges of the plates. Serve immediately.

Continued

1 cup extra-virgin olive oil

⅓ to ½ cup moscato vinegar

1 tablespoon roasted garlic
(see Note)

¼ cup black olive paste (tapenade;
see Note on page 35)

1 tablespoon minced capers

1 tablespoon minced sun-dried
tomatoes packed in oil, well drained

Salt and pepper

BLACK OLIVE VINAIGRETTE

Makes about 1¾ cups

Place the olive oil in a small mixing bowl. Whisk in the vinegar. When blended, whisk in the garlic, olive paste, capers, and tomatoes. When thoroughly combined, taste and, if necessary, adjust the seasoning with salt and pepper.

Use as directed in the recipe or cover and store, refrigerated, for up to 1 month. Bring to room temperature before using.

Note: To make roasted garlic or roasted garlic puree, lightly coat either un-peeled whole garlic heads or individual unpeeled cloves with olive oil and wrap in aluminum foil. Place on a rimmed baking sheet and bake in a preheated 350°F oven until soft and aromatic. Whole heads will take about 25 minutes and individual cloves about 12 minutes. The flesh can then easily be squeezed from the skin; it can be left whole or mashed to puree. One large head of garlic will usually yield about 2 tablespoons garlic puree.

CHAPTER 2

QUICK AND EASY **LUNCHES**

Lunch needs to be quick, simple, and get you to dinner. It is often difficult to maneuver a full lunch break during the week, but with a little bit of time, you can accomplish a lot. Sandwiches, like soups and salads, allow for spontaneity in putting together new combinations and tastes. Sometimes, something as simple as doctoring up mayonnaise with herbs and spices can turn an everyday sandwich into a savory meal. As delicious as my ratatouille and Brussels sprout gratin are alone, they also make spectacular sides for outdoor barbecues or even elegant dinners.

THREE FAVORITE
CHEESE SANDWICHES

Sometimes there is nothing better than a crispy, golden-brown crust with melted cheese—even the simple ones I grew up on, made with good ole American slices. But these days there is every reason to enjoy a sandwich with one of the local farmstead cheeses available across the country. Whether I am in California or New York, I can always make a truly great cheese sandwich for my family using locally produced cheese. I give you my versions of three delicious ones: one with aged Gouda, a Croque Monsieur, and an Italian-style—all family favorites. I like to serve a Brooklyn Lager with the Gouda sandwich, as the aging causes the cheese to have a slight caramel flavor and some crystallization, which seems to be accented by the caramel aroma of the lager.

You can turn the Croque Monsieur into a Croque Madame by topping it with one or two sunny-side-up eggs.

GRILLED AGED GOUDA SANDWICHES

Serves 6

12 thick slices brioche bread

About ¼ cup (½ stick) unsalted butter, at room temperature

18 thick slices aged Gouda cheese

Farmers market pickles for serving

Generously coat one side of each slice of brioche with butter. Place 3 slices of cheese on the buttered side of each of 6 slices. Place a slice of brioche, buttered side down, on top.

Heat a cast-iron skillet over medium heat until very hot but not smoking.

Lightly butter the outsides of two or three sandwiches and place in the hot skillet. Cook, turning occasionally, for about 7 minutes or until the bread is golden and crisp and the cheese has melted. Repeat to cook the remaining sandwiches.

Cut each sandwich in half on the diagonal and serve with some great farmers market pickles.

CROQUE MONSIEUR

Serves 6

---

12 thick slices rustic bread or home-style white bread

About 3 tablespoons salted butter, at room temperature

¼ cup Dijon mustard (or to taste)

18 slices hard cheese, such as Gruyère, Comté, provolone, mimolette, or aged cheddar

½ cup sliced sour pickles

12 slices fine-quality ham

Mornay Sauce (recipe follows)

---

2 cups whole milk

¼ cup (½ stick) unsalted butter

¼ cup all-purpose flour

1½ cups shredded hard cheese (traditionally it is Comté or Gruyère, but I suggest you use whatever hard farmstead cheese you like—Gouda-style works well, and my sons like cheddar)

Salt

Tabasco sauce

Preheat the oven to 450°F. Line a baking sheet with parchment paper or a silicone liner.

Generously coat one side of each slice of bread with butter. In batches, place the bread, buttered side down, in a large nonstick frying pan over medium heat. Cook for about 3 minutes or just until the buttered sides are golden brown.

Place 6 of the slices, buttered side down, on the prepared baking sheet and generously coat with mustard. Place 2 slices of cheese on each. Top with a layer of pickles, followed by 2 slices of ham. Top with another slice of cheese and a second slice of the toasted bread, buttered side up.

Using an offset spatula, spread an equal portion of the Mornay Sauce over the top of each sandwich. Bake for about 10 minutes or until the topping is golden brown and the cheese is bubbling out of the sides.

Cut each sandwich in half on the diagonal and serve.

MORNAY SAUCE

Makes about 3 cups

Bring the milk to a simmer in a small saucepan over medium heat. Remove from the heat and keep warm.

Melt the butter in a small saucepan over medium-low heat. When completely melted, add the flour, stirring to blend completely. Do not allow the mixture to color. When completely incorporated, whisk in the reserved warm milk. Whisking constantly, return to a simmer.

Add the cheese and continue to cook, stirring constantly, for about 4 minutes or until the cheese has melted completely and a smooth sauce has formed. Season with salt and Tabasco and set aside to cool for about 30 minutes or until thick enough to spread. (If you want to use this as a sauce in another dish, you may use it immediately.)

ITALIAN-STYLE GRILLED CHEESE SANDWICHES

3

Serves 6

12 thick slices ciabatta or
6 ciabatta rolls

¼ cup extra-virgin olive oil

⅓ cup black olive paste
(tapenade, see Note)

12 slices provolone cheese

3 ripe tomatoes, peeled, cored, and
cut crosswise into thin slices

¼ cup fresh basil leaves

12 slices smoked mozzarella cheese

2 teaspoons fresh oregano leaves

Pepper

Preheat the oven to 450°F. Line a baking sheet with parchment paper or a silicone liner.

Generously coat one side of each piece of bread with olive oil. Place 6 slices, oiled side down, on the prepared baking sheet. Lightly coat each of the 6 slices with olive paste. Top with 2 slices provolone cheese and a layer of tomatoes, followed by a layer of basil leaves. Top the basil with 2 slices of mozzarella cheese. Sprinkle with the oregano and pepper and top with a second slice of bread, oiled side up.

Bake for about 6 minutes or until the cheese is melting and the bottoms are golden brown. Carefully turn and bake for another 5 minutes or until both sides are golden brown and the cheese is melting. Serve immediately.

Note: Black olive paste (also known as tapenade) is sold in specialty food stores, many supermarkets, and online. You can also make your own simple tapenade by combining ½ pound pitted olives (black, green, or a mix) with 3 basil leaves, 2 well-drained anchovy fillets, 1 large clove garlic, ¼ cup extra-virgin olive oil, 2 tablespoons well-drained capers, 1 tablespoon lemon juice, and ½ teaspoon thyme leaves in the bowl of a food processor fitted with the metal blade. Process, using quick on-and-off turns, until coarsely ground. You don't want a puree, nor do you want big chunks of olives remaining.

I like to serve a Brooklyn Lager from the Brooklyn Brewery with the grilled Gouda sandwich. Artisanal beers have become big business in America with many young people going from college to brewing beer (perhaps because they have become experienced in drinking it during their college years). Brooklyn Brewery was one of the early artisanal breweries, founded in 1988. But beer had a long tradition in Brooklyn's history: In the 1800s Brooklyn was one of the largest brewing centers in the country and lager beer was a favorite. Brooklyn Lager is a rich amber-gold with lots of hop aroma and caramel flavors. The aromatic qualities are enhanced by "dry-hopping," a centuries-old practice of steeping the beer with fresh hops as it undergoes a long, cold maturation, which makes it a perfect go-with for all types of foods and, particularly, cheeses.

CRAB LOUIE TRIPLE-DECKER SANDWICHES

Serves 6

1½ pounds Dungeness or lump crabmeat, picked clean of all cartilage and shell

Green Goddess Dressing (recipe follows) or Thousand Island (or Russian) Dressing (page 18)

8 hard-boiled eggs, peeled

¼ cup chopped green olives

18 slices white bread, toasted

2 ripe beefsteak tomatoes, peeled, cored, and cut crosswise into thin slices

12 slices thick-sliced applewood-smoked bacon, cooked

6 large leaves iceberg lettuce

Crab Louie Salad is a San Francisco classic. When I was a visitor, I would always stop by Swan Oyster Depot on Polk Street for my fix. And it is from Swan's that I got my inspiration to take the classic salad and turn it into a club sandwich. Along with the crab, the salad components are iceberg lettuce, hard-boiled eggs, tomatoes, and, sometimes, olives—all of which contribute to a great club sandwich. The dressing can be either Louie (which is really Thousand Island or Russian dressing) or Green Goddess (my personal choice).

Place the crabmeat in a medium mixing bowl and add just enough dressing to moisten it. Set aside.

Place the eggs in a medium mixing bowl and, using a kitchen fork, smash them into large chunks. Add the olives along with just enough dressing to hold the mixture together.

Lay 6 slices of toast on a clean work surface. Spread each one with a nice coating of the dressing. Mound an equal portion of the crab mixture on each slice. Top with a couple of tomato slices.

Lightly coat both sides of 6 slices of toast with a thin layer of the dressing. Place one slice on top of the crab. Top it with a layer of the egg mixture and then with 2 slices of bacon and a leaf of lettuce.

Lightly coat one side of the final 6 slices of toast with the dressing. Place the toast on each stacked sandwich on top of the lettuce, dressing side down, pushing slightly to hold the stack together.

Using a serrated knife, cut each sandwich into 4 equal triangles. Insert a toothpick (for the diner touch, make it a frilly one) into each triangle to hold it together. Serve immediately.

Continued

1 cup mayonnaise

½ cup fresh buttermilk

2 anchovy fillets packed in oil,
well drained and finely chopped

1 clove garlic, finely minced

¼ cup mixed chopped fresh herbs,
such as chives, flat-leaf parsley,
and tarragon

¼ cup chopped scallion greens

1 teaspoon fresh lemon juice

Salt and pepper

GREEN GODDESS DRESSING

Makes about 2 cups

Combine the mayonnaise and buttermilk in a small mixing bowl. Add the anchovies, garlic, herbs, scallion greens, and lemon juice, stirring until well combined. Taste and season with salt and pepper.

Serve immediately or store, covered and refrigerated, for up to 3 days.

REUBEN SANDWICHES

Serves 6

1 loaf seedless rye bread

2 cups Thousand Island (or Russian) Dressing (page 18)

2 pounds warm corned beef or brisket, sliced

12 ounces sauerkraut

12 thick slices raclette or other semi-hard Swiss cheese

3 tablespoons salted butter, melted

Dill pickles for serving

This is a classic New York City deli sandwich. It really is at its best when it's piled high with rich, fatty corned beef—the hallmark of a great Jewish delicatessen. I often cook up a corned beef just to make these sandwiches so that we can experience the required juiciness and flavor. The warmth of the meat sends juices right into the rye bread for a remarkable texture.

Preheat the oven to 450°F.

Using a bread knife, cut the bread on the diagonal into 12 slices.

Lay the bread slices on a flat work surface. Generously coat one side of each piece with dressing. Pile an equal portion of the corned beef on 6 of the slices. Top the meat with sauerkraut followed by 2 slices of cheese. Place a remaining slice of bread on top, dressing side down.

Using a pastry brush, generously coat both sides of the sandwiches with melted butter. Place the sandwiches on a baking sheet. If you have some heavy ovenproof pans (cast-iron skillets work well), you can place a weight on top of the sandwiches to press them down—this does help the finished sandwich hold together. Bake for about 5 minutes or until the bottoms are toasted and the cheese begins to melt. Using a spatula, turn and toast on the remaining side for another 5 minutes or until well toasted and the cheese has melted completely.

Cut the sandwiches in half on the diagonal, and serve with dill pickles and extra dressing on the side.

SMOKED SALMON
PLATTER

Serves 6

1 sourdough baguette

6 leaves Bibb lettuce

1 avocado, pitted, peeled, and cut lengthwise into 6 wedges

6 slices smoked salmon

12 very thin small tomato slices

Thin slices red onion, halved

About 1½ tablespoons lemon-scented olive oil

Sea salt and cracked black pepper

4 or 5 fresh chives, cut into 1-inch lengths

Lunch or brunch, or even a late-night supper? A smoked salmon platter fills the bill for all of those occasions. I give the kids the job of making the toasts; they love how the thin slices of bread curl as they toast. I have given the proportions for 6 toast bundles, but, to be honest, everyone has more than one, so I usually slice and toast the whole baguette and have plenty of the other components on hand for seconds and thirds.

Preheat the oven to 350°F. Line a baking sheet with parchment paper.

Using a sharp knife, cut the baguette on the diagonal into very thin slices—absolutely as thin as you can make them. (The thinner they are, the more likely they are to create the desired curl around the edges during baking so that the toasts make an almost basket shape.)

Place the bread slices on the prepared baking sheet and bake for about 6 minutes or until the thin toasts are golden brown and beginning to curl up around the edges. Let cool.

Place 6 slices of toast on a platter. Top each one with a lettuce leaf, followed by a wedge of avocado, a slice of salmon, 2 slices of tomato, and 2 or 3 pieces of red onion. Drizzle the oil over the top of each toast bundle. Season with sea salt and cracked black pepper and garnish with a few chive pieces.

Serve with extra toasts on the side, if desired.

Wine Pairing: My exclusive sparkling wine, Aureole Cuvée from Iron Horse Vineyards (chardonnay and pinot grapes). Festive and gala-worthy, it is the wine that I always serve with smoked salmon.

WOOD-ROASTED
CHIPOTLE OYSTERS

Serves 6

3 dozen oysters

Rock salt (see Note)

Chipotle Butter (recipe follows)

½ cup fresh bread crumbs

The boys first experienced oysters roasted on the half shell at the Hog Island Oyster Co. in Marshall, not too far from our home in Healdsburg. I didn't think that they would take to the taste as quickly as they did, but boy, did they. And once I prepared oysters on our wood-fired grill, they quickly became a preferred lunch. A glass of chilled muscadet (see Wine Pairing) is called for to celebrate the briny oysters.

If you are lucky enough to have one, build a hot fire in a wood-fired oven; alternatively, preheat a charcoal grill to high or preheat the oven to 400°F.

Using a stiff kitchen scrub brush, scrub each oyster under cold running water to clean thoroughly.

Line 2 shallow baking dishes (we use a 6-quart Staub cocotte or casserole) or rimmed baking sheets with a ½-inch layer of rock salt (see page 44). Set aside.

Place an even layer of the salt on a serving platter large enough to hold the oysters. This will be used to serve the oysters. Set aside.

Place a thick glove on your nondominant hand and an oyster-shucking knife in your dominant hand. Working with one oyster at a time, place it in the palm of your gloved hand and hold on to it. With the oyster level with the shucking knife, insert the tip of the knife in between the shell next to the hinge at the back. Using the knife as leverage, twist into the shell to pry it apart. You will hear a sharp noise as the shell opens. Do not force it open or the shell will crack. Holding the oyster firmly and evenly, gently twist the knife to open the shell entirely. Still keeping the bottom shell level (you don't want to lose any of the juice), cut the muscle at the hinge to detach and loosen the oyster from the bottom shell. Discard the top shell.

Nestle the oyster half-shell into the salt on a prepared baking sheet and continue opening oysters until all are open.

When all of the oysters have been opened, place a slice of Chipotle Butter on top of each one and sprinkle with bread crumbs.

No matter which cooking method you use, keep the oysters on the salt-lined baking sheet and transfer to the preheated oven or grill. Quickly cover the grill. Bake or grill for about 7 minutes or until the

oysters are curling slightly, the butter has melted, and the bread crumbs are golden and crisp. In either case, you don't want to lose any of the oyster liquor as the butter melts into it, creating a delicious sauce.

Transfer the roasted oysters to the salt-lined serving platter and serve, 6 per person, piping hot.

Note: If you don't have rock salt or can't find it, you can use an equal amount of coarse or kosher salt.

CHIPOTLE BUTTER

Makes 1½ cups

1½ cups (3 sticks) unsalted butter, at room temperature

4 chipotle chiles in adobo, stemmed and seeded

2 tablespoons lemon juice

½ teaspoon ground cumin

Salt and cayenne pepper

Combine the butter, chiles, lemon juice, cumin, salt, and cayenne in the bowl of a food processor fitted with the metal blade and process to thoroughly blend.

Using a rubber spatula, scrape the butter mixture into the center of a piece of plastic wrap (or waxed paper). Fold the wrap over the butter and, using your hands, form the butter into a neat log about 1½ inches in diameter. Tightly close the ends of the plastic wrap and transfer the log to the refrigerator. Chill for at least 1 hour or until firm, or freeze for up to 3 months.

When ready to use, unwrap the log and cut the butter, crosswise, into ¼-inch thick slices. Use as directed.

Hog Island Oyster Farm is located on the eastern shores of Tomales Bay, about an hour's drive from San Francisco. Early on they were participants in the local/sustainable/farm-to-table movement in California, having raised naturally sustainable oysters, Manila clams, and mussels for over 30 years. The farm is open to the public, and the complete farm-to-plate oyster experience is offered to visitors. You can shuck your own oysters or have them do it for you; either way, it is a delicious way to spend an afternoon.

Wine Pairing: Muscadet, a recent rediscovery for me. It is a light-bodied wine that is refreshing and crisp and marries well with almost all shellfish.

WOOD-ROASTED LEMON–**RED CHILE SHRIMP** WITH CABBAGE SALAD

Serves 6

2 pounds jumbo (U15) shrimp (see Note)

Grated zest and juice of 1 lemon

½ cup olive oil

2 hot red chiles, stemmed and cut crosswise into thin slices

2 shallots, minced

Salt and pepper

2 tablespoons unsalted butter

½ cup chopped scallions

2 tablespoons chopped fresh flat-leaf parsley or cilantro

Cabbage Salad (recipe follows)

Sourdough bread for serving

I like to use big, fat heads-on shrimp for this dish and let everyone peel their own at the table. This, of course, works best when we're dining outdoors. You don't really need to make the salad to complete the meal, but I find it a refreshing accompaniment to the spicy shrimp. An artisanal sparkling cider works very well as the drink of choice with shrimp as it holds up to the spice and citrus.

If you are lucky enough to have one, build a hot fire in a wood-fired oven; alternatively, preheat the oven to 450°F.

Combine the shrimp with the lemon zest and juice, olive oil, chiles, and shallots in a roasting pan. Cover with plastic wrap and allow to marinate for 15 minutes.

Uncover, season with salt and pepper, and roast for about 8 minutes or until the shrimp are bright pink.

Stir in the butter, scallions, and parsley. Serve immediately with the salad on the side and some warm sourdough bread to sop up the juices.

Note: In California I have learned that small shrimp are called "shrimp" and large ones "prawns," while in New York all sizes are called shrimp. For simplicity, I stick with the New York terminology. The numbers that follow a pound of shrimp indicate how many you can expect to be in a pound of a given size—U15 simply means that a pound will yield 15 or under meaty shrimp. (The "U" stands for "under.")

Continued

½ large green cabbage, cored
and julienned

1 red onion

1 bulb fennel, trimmed
of tough stalks

2 teaspoons grated lemon zest

5 tablespoons lemon juice

1 teaspoon Dijon mustard

1 cup extra-virgin olive oil

Salt and pepper

CABBAGE SALAD

Serves 6

Place the cabbage in a large salad bowl.

Peel the onion and cut lengthwise in half. Cut each half crosswise into very thin slices. Add the onion to the cabbage.

Trim the fennel of any brown spots and cut lengthwise in half. Remove the core and cut each half crosswise into very thin slices. Add the fennel to the cabbage and onion, tossing to blend the vegetables together.

Combine the lemon zest, juice, and mustard in a small mixing bowl, whisking to blend well. Slowly add the oil, whisking until well emulsified. Season with salt and pepper. Pour the dressing over the cabbage mixture, tossing to blend well.

QUICK AND EASY **PIZZA**

Makes one 15-inch pizza

3 cups 00 flour (see Note)
2 teaspoons sugar
2 teaspoons salt
2 (¼-ounce) packages instant or RapidRise yeast
1⅓ cups warm water
4 tablespoons extra-virgin olive oil
1½ cups shredded mozzarella
1 basket heirloom cherry tomatoes, cut in half lengthwise
¾ cup pitted black olives
1 teaspoon fresh rosemary needles, optional
1 teaspoon red chile flakes (or to taste), optional
1 cup grated Parmesan cheese

This is about the easiest and quickest pizza dough I've found. And once you've got it in your repertoire, you can make almost any kind of pizza you like—from a traditional margherita to a breakfast pizza with Gruyère, prosciutto or other ham, tomatoes, and a few eggs cracked onto the top. With this dough, all types of cheeses and meats and sauces have a welcome mat, so when you want to make innovative pizzas, this is the place to begin.

Although I am lucky enough to have a wood-fired oven, a very hot home oven can brown and crisp the crust very well. Or, I've seen relatively inexpensive outdoor, gas-fired pizza ovens at Williams-Sonoma (see Sources, page 243).

Coat the interior of a large bowl with olive oil. Set aside.

Combine the flour, sugar, and salt in a mixing bowl. Add the yeast, stirring to blend in. Combine the water with 2 tablespoons of the olive oil. Pour the water mixture into the flour mixture, beating to combine. When blended, scrape the dough onto a lightly floured surface and knead with your hands for about 5 minutes or until smooth and elastic. Transfer the dough to the oiled bowl, cover, and let rest for 20 minutes.

If you are lucky enough to have one, build a hot fire in a wood-fired oven; alternatively, preheat the oven to 450°F. Lightly coat a 10- by 15-inch rimmed baking sheet with olive oil.

Lightly flour a clean, flat work surface. You can also dust it with semolina flour if you have it on hand.

Scrape the dough out onto the floured surface and, using a rolling pin, roll it out to about a 12- by 16-inch rectangle. Lift the dough up and fit it into the oiled pan, taking care to push the dough up against all sides of the pan.

Sprinkle the top with the mozzarella. Randomly place the tomatoes over the cheese. Place the olives on the cheese and, if using, sprinkle the rosemary and chile flakes over the top. Drizzle the remaining 2 tablespoons olive oil over the top and then sprinkle with the grated Parmesan.

Bake for about 15 minutes or until the cheese is melted and bubbly, the tomatoes slightly charred, and the dough cooked through and golden brown.

Let the pizza rest for about 5 minutes before cutting into slices.

Note: "00 flour" is a finely ground Italian flour with a very light texture that is traditionally used to make pizza and pasta dough. It is very easy to work with and gives the perfect mouth-feel to pasta dough once cooked. It is lower in protein and softer than American all-purpose or bread flour. The "00" is an Italian grading that refers to the grind and almost pure white color, in addition to how much of the bran and germ has been removed during milling. It is available at Italian markets, specialty food stores, many supermarkets, and online through King Arthur Flour (see Sources, page 243).

CHARLIE'S PESTO FLATBREAD

Serves 8

3 cups whole wheat flour

½ teaspoon instant or RapidRise yeast

2 teaspoons salt

1½ cups water

6 tablespoons extra-virgin olive oil, plus more for drizzling

Semolina or Wondra flour for rolling out the dough

Basil Pesto (see Note at Mint Pesto, page 6)

1½ cups shredded scamorza (dry mozzarella)

¾ cup chopped pine nuts

2 ripe tomatoes, peeled, cored, and cut into thin wedges

1 cup shredded romaine lettuce

1 cup grated Parmesan cheese

Flatbreads are less than pizza and more than a cracker, particularly when coated with interesting toppings. They are terrific to serve with cocktails or chilled wine on a summer afternoon or around the fire in the winter. I like to serve them straight from my wood-fired oven. I quickly use a Microplane to grate the Parmesan over the salad-topped hot flatbread and then place it on a cutting board with a big knife so that everyone can cut their own randomly shaped piece.

Lightly coat the interior of a large bowl with olive oil. Set aside.

Combine the flour with the yeast in the bowl of a standing electric mixer fitted with the dough hook. Stir in the salt. Add the water along with the olive oil and beat on low for about 5 minutes or until a smooth dough forms. Transfer to the oiled bowl, loosely cover, and set aside in a warm spot for 20 minutes or until the dough is just slightly risen.

Place a pizza stone in the oven and preheat the oven to 400°F.

Lightly coat a clean, flat work surface with semolina or Wondra flour.

Transfer the dough to the floured surface. Using a rolling pin, roll the dough out to a large thin, round. It doesn't have to be even; you want a rustic look.

Using a pastry brush, generously coat the top of the dough with pesto. Sprinkle with scamorza and pine nuts. Using a pizza peel, transfer the flatbread to the stone in the preheated oven. Bake for about 12 minutes or until the topping is bubbling and the crust is crisp and golden brown.

Remove from the oven and randomly top with tomato wedges and romaine. Drizzle olive oil over all and sprinkle with Parmesan cheese. Serve immediately.

BAKED **RATATOUILLE**

Serves 6 to 8

½ cup extra-virgin olive oil

1 large red onion, cut into large dice

1 tablespoon minced garlic

3 pounds Japanese eggplant, trimmed and cut into large dice

1 large zucchini, trimmed and cut into large dice

1 large yellow summer squash, trimmed and cut into large dice

1 (28-ounce) can chopped San Marzano tomatoes with their juice

2 tablespoons chopped fresh basil

Salt and pepper

1½ pounds mozzarella cheese, thinly sliced

½ cup grated Parmesan cheese

⅓ cup fresh bread crumbs

This is a dish that I make all summer long when the farmers market is filled with eggplant and summer squashes. It is based on the traditional French Provençal vegetable dish that usually includes bell peppers and a mixture of dried herbs. You really can do anything you want with it: Some cooks prepare each vegetable separately and then mix together, while some layer the vegetables and bake them. Once baked, my version can be eaten hot, warm, or cold as a side dish; incorporated into salads, frittatas, and pastas; or packed into a crusty roll for a delicious vegetarian sandwich. You can use equal amounts of each vegetable or more or less of each one—make it to your own taste.

Preheat the oven to 350°F. Lightly coat the interior of a large ceramic baking dish with olive oil.

Heat the olive oil in a large saucepan over medium heat. Add the onion and garlic and cook, stirring frequently, for about 5 minutes or just until soft. Add the eggplant and continue to cook, stirring frequently, for about 15 minutes or until just beginning to soften. Stir in the zucchini and yellow squash and cook, stirring frequently, for another 10 minutes or until just barely tender. Stir in the tomatoes and basil and season with salt and pepper.

Scrape about half of the eggplant mixture into the prepared baking dish. Cover with half of the mozzarella. Spoon the remaining eggplant mixture over the cheese. Top with another layer of mozzarella. Sprinkle the Parmesan over the mozzarella and then top with the bread crumbs.

Bake for about 35 minutes or until the top is golden brown and the cheese is bubbling. Serve hot, warm, or at room temperature.

BRUSSELS SPROUT
AND RICOTTA GRATIN

Serves 6

2½ cups (about 1¼ pounds)
fresh ricotta cheese
(see Fresh Ricotta, page 56)

3 large eggs, at room temperature

2 cups whole milk

1 teaspoon grated lemon zest

1 cup grated Parmesan cheese

Salt and pepper

About 24 Brussels sprouts,
cut in half lengthwise

2 teaspoons fresh thyme leaves

If your family doesn't like Brussels sprouts, this gratin will convince them that they really do love them. It is important to use a really good fresh ricotta as it adds a richness and creaminess not found in commercially packed ricottas. In California, I use ricotta from Bellwether Farms in Sonoma, and in New York I find my fresh ricotta at Di Palo's Fine Foods on Grand Street (see Sources, page 243). And if you are particularly adventuresome, you can easily make fresh ricotta at home (page 56).

Preheat the oven to 350°F. Lightly coat the interior of a shallow 3-quart glass or ceramic baking dish with butter.

Combine the ricotta with the eggs, milk, and lemon zest in a large mixing bowl, beating to blend. Fold in the Parmesan and season with salt and pepper.

Pour the mixture into the prepared baking dish. Arrange the Brussels sprouts, cut side up, in the cheese mixture. Sprinkle the top with the thyme.

Bake for about 45 minutes or until the Brussels sprouts are cooked and lightly colored and the cheese is bubbling and brown around the edges. Serve hot.

Continued

Fresh Ricotta

If you want to make fresh ricotta, here's what you do: Line a strainer with 3 layers of moist cheesecloth and set over a large glass bowl. Combine 2 cups whole milk, 1 cup heavy cream, 1½ tablespoons white vinegar, and ½ teaspoon salt (or less or more, depending on your taste) in a 4-cup glass measuring cup. Microwave on high for about 3 minutes or until the milk is just beginning to bubble and it registers 165°F on an instant-read thermometer. Using a wooden spoon, gently stir for 5 seconds. You will see the mixture begin to separate into solid curds and opaque liquid (the whey). If this doesn't occur, microwave on high for an additional 30 seconds or until the separation is evident. (If you don't have a microwave, place the milk, cream, and salt in a heavy-bottomed pot over medium heat and bring to a boil. Cook at a full boil for 1 minute. Remove from the heat and stir in the vinegar. Then let the mixture rest for about 1 minute or just until it separates into curds and whey.) Using a slotted spoon, transfer the curds to the cheesecloth-lined strainer, cover with plastic wrap, and set aside to drain for about 25 minutes or until the desired consistency is reached. The longer you allow the mixture to drain, the denser the finished cheese. Transfer to a nonreactive container and store, covered and refrigerated, for up to 5 days.

CHEESE STRATA

Serves 6 to 8

5 cups stale French bread cubes (include some crust)

2 cups shredded Monterey Jack cheese

1½ cups diced smoked ham

10 large eggs

3 cups milk

1 cup heavy cream

¼ cup finely minced onion

2 tablespoons chopped fresh chives

1 teaspoon dry mustard powder

1 teaspoon Worcestershire sauce

¼ teaspoon smoked paprika

Salt and pepper

We almost always have some leftover baguette in the house, and this is a great way to put it to good use. I put the entire dish together the night before a football game and pop it into the oven for lunch the next day. You can use any type of cheese, any vegetable, such as chopped broccoli, spinach, or bell pepper, or any meat that works well with eggs, such as bacon, sausage, or cured meat. My mom made a very simple version with Velveeta that we all called "Mom's cheese dish," and I would bet that most other American families also have a version of their own.

Generously coat the interior of a 9- by 13-inch baking dish with unsalted butter. Scatter the bread cubes over the bottom of the dish and then sprinkle the cheese and ham over the bread cubes.

Combine the eggs, milk, heavy cream, onion, chives, mustard, Worcestershire sauce, and paprika in a large mixing bowl, whisking to blend well. Season with salt and pepper and pour over the mixture in the baking dish. Cover with plastic wrap and refrigerate for 4 hours or up to 24 hours.

When ready to bake, preheat the oven to 350°F.

Remove the covered dish from the refrigerator and take off and discard the plastic wrap. Bake for 1 hour or until the strata has puffed up, the center is set, and the top is golden brown. If the top begins to get too brown before the center is setting, tent the dish with aluminum foil.

Place on a wire rack to cool for about 10 minutes before serving.

PORK AND KIDNEY BEAN **CHILI**

Serves 6 to 8 with leftovers

1 pound dried kidney beans

1 tablespoon canola oil

2½ pounds lean pork, cut into small cubes

1 large onion, chopped

1 red bell pepper, cored, seeded, membrane removed, and diced

1 jalapeño chile, stemmed, seeded, and minced

1 tablespoon minced garlic

¼ cup chile powder

1 tablespoon ground cumin

2 teaspoons dried oregano (Mexican is great if you can find it)

1 teaspoon red pepper flakes (or to taste)

2 (28-ounce) cans chopped tomatoes, with their juice

2 cups tomato puree

1 tablespoon tomato paste

Salt and pepper

3 tablespoons chopped fresh cilantro

My style of chili has lots of meat and kidney beans, while Texas-style has no meat at all and usually features pinto beans. It doesn't matter which style you like, chilies are all delicious, filling, and even better after a few days in the fridge. Since we are a family of football fanatics, chili is an easy dish to keep on hand for football Sundays. I always have dried beans in the pantry, usually those from Rancho Gordo (see Sources, page 243), so I can get the soak started when I have other things to do and then throw the chili together quickly the next morning. Lots of cooks don't feel that the soaking step is necessary, so they boil dried beans for an hour and then proceed with a recipe. I do not like firm beans, so I follow the old rule of soaking in cool water for at least 8 hours.

I serve chili with some diced Maui onion on top; I love the contrast of the crisp, cool sweetness with the spicy chili. You can also sprinkle with Monterey Jack or cheddar cheese or garnish with a scoop of sour cream and some chopped cilantro.

Place the beans in a large soup pot and cover with cold water by 2 inches. Cover and set aside to soak for at least 8 hours or overnight.

Drain the beans, return to the pot, and add cold water to cover by 3 inches. Place over high heat and bring to a boil. Lower the heat and cook at a bare simmer.

While the beans simmer, heat the oil in a large frying pan over medium-high heat. Add the pork, onion, bell pepper, chile, and garlic. Cook, stirring frequently, for about 15 minutes or until the meat has browned and the onion has taken on some color.

Once the pork is browned, scrape the pork mixture into the pot, along with the chile powder, cumin, oregano, and, if using, the red pepper flakes. Simmer for another 30 minutes.

Add the tomatoes and their juice, the tomato puree, and the tomato paste, stirring to blend very well. Season with salt and pepper and continue to simmer for about 1 hour or until the mixture is very flavorful and the beans are tender.

Remove from the heat, stir in the cilantro, and serve.

CHAPTER 3

VEGETABLES AND SIDES

I've never understood how anyone could not like vegetables. When I was a kid we didn't really have a large selection to choose from, since our growing season was so short in upstate New York. As a chef, I have access to literally anything that's grown, but nothing is better than simple and basic vegetable preparation. Three important vegetable principles to live by: Use local produce, use in-season produce, and use responsibly grown produce.

SPICED SWEET POTATOES

Serves 6

3 pounds small sweet potatoes or yams

¼ cup olive oil

1 teaspoon cayenne pepper

1 teaspoon sumac powder (see Note)

Salt

Juice of 1 lemon, optional

The sweetness of the potatoes is a great match for the spice of the cayenne and the acidity of the sumac. I think these are a terrific alternative to French fries, as well as a healthy snack. Best of all, they are a marriage made in heaven when combined with most pork dishes.

Preheat the oven to 400°F. Line 2 rimmed baking sheets with parchment paper.

Scrub the sweet potatoes well and dry with a clean kitchen towel. Cut each in half lengthwise, and then cut each half into thin wedges. Place the sweet potatoes in a large bowl, add the olive oil, cayenne, sumac, and salt to taste, and toss to coat well.

Transfer the seasoned potato wedges to the prepared baking sheets, laying them out in a single layer with space in between.

Bake for about 15 minutes or until the bottoms are turning brown and beginning to crisp. Turn the slices and bake for an additional 12 minutes or just until the potatoes are crisp.

Serve hot, drizzled with lemon juice if desired.

Note: Sumac powder is the reddish-purple ground spice of the sumac berry. It adds bright color and tart flavor to many dishes, but the powder is specifically used in Middle Eastern and Greek cooking as both a garnish and a flavoring. In early American culinary history, it was used throughout Appalachia. Today ground sumac is used to make a refreshing and cooling summer drink called rhus juice. The spice is available at Middle Eastern markets, specialty food stores, and online.

STEAK HOUSE POTATOES

Serves 6

5 large Idaho potatoes,
well scrubbed

½ cup olive oil

1 tablespoon chopped fresh
rosemary, optional

1 teaspoon paprika

Salt and pepper

Here is another alternative to French fries: easy, quick, and healthy, too. These "fries" are a great side for almost any grilled or roasted meat and the best accompaniment for burgers and grilled steaks. You will find them so tasty that you won't need ketchup.

Preheat the oven to 400°F. Generously oil 2 large rimmed baking sheets.

Using a sharp knife, cut each potato in half lengthwise and then cut each half into thick wedges. Place in a large bowl, drizzle the oil over the potatoes, and then sprinkle with the rosemary if using and the paprika. Season with salt and pepper and toss to coat each wedge evenly.

Place the seasoned wedges in a single layer on the prepared sheets; you don't want to crowd the potatoes as you want them to crisp on all sides. Roast, turning occasionally, for about 24 minutes or until the potatoes are golden brown and crispy.

TEMPURA
ONION RINGS

Serves 6

Vegetable oil for frying

2 large onions, cut crosswise
into ½-inch-thick slices

3 cups all-purpose flour

½ cup rice flour

2 teaspoons salt

½ teaspoon baking soda

1½ cups seltzer water

1½ cups light beer

Salt and pepper

The boys first discovered onion rings at a beach shack serving those not-too-wonderful frozen battered rings deep-fried in old oil. You can still find them at ice cream stands and fast-food stalls at beaches (lake and ocean) all across the country. Like all kids, they loved the crisp exterior and slightly greasy salty slick to be licked off their fingers. Rather than ban them, I made onion rings at home to let them know that onion rings can be great.

Preheat the oven to 200°F. Place a wire rack on a baking sheet and line another baking sheet with a double layer of paper towels.

Heat the oil in a large deep-fat fryer or large deep saucepan over medium heat to 365°F on a candy thermometer.

Pull the onions apart into rings, taking care to remove and discard any of the thin, wet membranes that separate the rings. Set the rings aside.

Combine 2 cups of the all-purpose flour with the rice flour, salt, and baking soda in a large mixing bowl, stirring to blend. Whisk in the seltzer and beer, beating until a smooth batter forms.

Place the remaining 1 cup of flour in a large shallow bowl.

Working with one at a time, dust an onion ring in the flour and then dip into the batter, lifting up and allowing the excess batter to drip off.

Drop the coated onion ring into the hot oil and fry for about 2 minutes or until golden brown on the bottom. Using a skimmer, lift the onion ring and turn it over to fry for about 1 minute longer or until golden. You can fry a few rings at a time, but don't crowd the fryer.

When they are golden, use the skimmer to transfer the rings to the paper towel–lined baking sheet to drain. Season with salt and pepper. Once drained, transfer to the rack on the baking sheet and place in the oven to keep warm until all of the rings have been fried.

PARSNIP AND
CELERY ROOT PUREE

Serves 6

3 large parsnips, peeled
and cubed

1 large (about 2½ pounds)
celery root, peeled, trimmed,
and cubed

1½ cups chicken stock or canned
nonfat, low-sodium chicken broth

Salt

¾ cup crème fraîche

2 tablespoons unsalted butter

1 tablespoon grated orange zest

White pepper

This combination of frequently unused vegetables makes for a rich and satisfying side dish that will have everyone asking for seconds. For an even richer dish, cook the vegetables in milk and butter, but still add the crème fraîche and butter at the end. A bit of an overload, but very, very delicious nonetheless.

Combine the parsnips and celery root with the chicken stock in a large saucepan. Season with salt, place over medium heat, and bring to a simmer. Cover and simmer for about 18 minutes or until the vegetables are very soft.

Drain well, reserving any cooking liquid.

Place the vegetables in the bowl of a food processor fitted with the metal blade. Add the crème fraîche and butter and process to a smooth puree, adding as much of the reserved cooking liquid as necessary to smooth the mixture.

Scrape into a serving bowl, fold in the orange zest, and season with white pepper. Taste and, if necessary, adjust the salt. Serve immediately, or store, covered and refrigerated, until ready to use. Reheat in the top half of a double boiler (or a microwave) before serving.

SLOW-ROASTED
FENNEL WITH DILL

Serves 6

5 medium fennel bulbs

Grated zest of 1 orange

Smoked paprika (to taste)

Salt

¼ cup extra-virgin olive oil

4 cloves garlic, cut into slivers

¼ cup chicken stock or
canned nonfat, low-sodium
chicken broth

3 tablespoons chopped fresh dill

Juice of 1 lemon

Cracked black pepper

I've always been partial to fennel. Because of its tart licorice-like flavor and crispness, I frequently use it raw in salads, but when it is slowly braised or roasted, fennel becomes very sweet. Fresh dill carries some of the same flavor notes as fennel, so they work particularly well together.

Preheat the oven to 325°F.

Trim the tough stalks from the fennel, discarding the stalks but reserving the feathery fronds. Chop the fronds and set them aside for garnish. Trim any brown spots from the fennel and then cut each bulb lengthwise into 6 equal wedges. Place the fennel in a large bowl and add the orange zest, paprika, and salt. Toss to season well.

Place the oil and slivered garlic in a large shallow glass or ceramic baking dish. Add the fennel, cut sides down. Roast, turning the fennel occasionally, for about 30 minutes or until the fennel is golden and caramelized.

Raise the oven temperature to 400°F. Add the stock and dill to the fennel and continue to roast for another 12 minutes or until the liquid has almost evaporated and the fennel is cooked through.

Drizzle lemon juice over the fennel, sprinkle with the cracked black pepper and the chopped fennel fronds, and serve directly from the baking dish.

PROSCIUTTO-WRAPPED
ZUCCHINI

Serves 6

3 large zucchini

1 tablespoon extra-virgin olive oil, plus more for drizzling

1 large onion, finely diced

2 teaspoons minced garlic

Salt and pepper

¾ cup fresh bread crumbs

1 tablespoon finely chopped fresh basil

1½ cups (about 5 ounces) diced mozzarella cheese

6 ounces thinly sliced prosciutto

Cracked black pepper

This is another way to get people to eat (and enjoy) their vegetables. Zucchini is so mildly flavored that the cheese and ham add enough oomph to hide the fact that it is a vegetable at all. Plus, the prosciutto wrapping turns the plain squash into quite an elegant presentation. It goes particularly well with a grilled veal chop.

Preheat the oven to 450°F. Lightly coat the interior of a roasting pan with olive oil.

Trim each zucchini to about 7 inches long. Cut each one in half lengthwise. Using a scoop or a teaspoon, scoop out and reserve the center, leaving a shell about ¼ inch thick. Finely chop the flesh and set the shells aside.

Heat the olive oil in a large frying pan over medium heat. Add the onion and garlic and cook, stirring frequently, for about 5 minutes or until they have sweat their liquid and are tender. Stir in the chopped zucchini flesh, season with salt and pepper, and cook, stirring, for another 3 minutes or until the zucchini is tender.

Remove from the heat and stir in the bread crumbs and basil. Stir in the mozzarella. Working quickly (before the mozzarella has a chance to melt much), fill each zucchini shell with an equal portion of the stuffing, mounding slightly in the center. Working with one piece at a time, carefully wrap each stuffed zucchini with prosciutto, taking care that the entire zucchini is covered. As wrapped, place in the prepared roasting pan.

Drizzle the tops with extra-virgin olive oil and season with cracked black pepper. Bake for about 20 minutes or until the squash is just barely cooked and the prosciutto is nicely browned. Serve, one per person, hot or at room temperature.

SHISHITO PEPPERS
AND MUSHROOMS

Serves 6

1 pound shishito peppers, well washed, with the stems left on

1 tablespoon walnut oil

1 teaspoon grapeseed oil

¾ pound chanterelles or other wild mushrooms, cleaned and sliced

Tamari to taste (See Note)

½ cup chopped toasted walnuts

Shishito peppers, an import from Japan, where they are much esteemed, have only recently become available in the United States. They are particularly interesting because only occasionally does one carry heat. We find eating them is a game, as you never know when you will hit a hot one.

Using the point of a small sharp knife, poke a tiny hole into each pepper. This will keep them from popping open as they heat up.

Combine the walnut oil and grapeseed oil in a large frying pan over medium heat. Add the peppers and mushrooms and cook, tossing frequently with tongs, for about 20 minutes or until the peppers and mushrooms have taken on a little color and are tender.

Remove from the heat and season with tamari to taste. Add the walnuts and toss to combine. Transfer to a serving bowl and serve warm or at room temperature.

Note: Tamari is a soy-based sauce made primarily with soybeans with little or no wheat added. It is mellower, thicker, richer, and less salty than standard soy sauce, but if you don't have it on hand, soy sauce can be used in its place.

ROASTED EGGPLANT, CARROTS, AND ONION

Serves 6

1 large or 2 small eggplants

3 medium carrots

1 large sweet onion, unpeeled, halved crosswise

3 cloves garlic, unpeeled

3 tablespoons extra-virgin olive oil, plus more for rubbing the vegetables

Juice of 1 lemon

2 tablespoons tahini (sesame seed paste)

Cayenne pepper

Salt and pepper

2 tablespoons chopped fresh mint leaves

This is an intriguing combination of flavors. The grilled carrots add a sweetness that offsets the slight bitterness of the eggplant, while the onion and garlic add a hint of pungency. If you like, you can puree the mix and use it as a base for any grilled chop or a chicken breast. Or, use it as a dip with pita bread or crackers.

Preheat and oil the grill. (Alternatively, preheat the oven to 450°F.)

Rub the eggplants, carrots, onion, and garlic with oil. Wrap the garlic in aluminum foil. Place the eggplants and carrots on the hot grill. Add the onion halves, cut sides down. Place the wrapped garlic on the cooler side of the grill. Cover and grill, turning occasionally, for about 25 minutes or until the carrots and onion are charred and tender, the eggplant is charred and meltingly soft, and the garlic is soft. (Or place the vegetables on rimmed baking sheets and roast in the oven for approximately 25 minutes.) Split the eggplants in half and, using a large spoon, scrape the flesh from the skin into a large bowl; discard the skins.

Using your fingertips, push the peel from the carrots. Using a sharp knife, finely chop the carrots and add them to the eggplant.

Peel the outer charred skin from the onion and, using a sharp knife, finely chop. Add to the eggplant mix.

Unwrap the garlic and squeeze the flesh from the skin into the eggplant mix.

Add the lemon juice, the 3 tablespoons of extra-virgin olive oil, tahini, cayenne, and salt and pepper to taste. Using a rubber spatula, gently lift and fold to blend. When just about blended, add the mint and again fold to blend.

Serve warm or at room temperature.

GRILLED ROMAINE
WITH JACK CHEESE

Serves 6

---

3 hearts of romaine lettuce

About 6 tablespoons
extra-virgin olive oil

Salt and cracked black pepper

⅓ cup malt vinegar

½ cup crumbled dry Jack
cheese or other firm cheese
(see Vella Cheese, below)

Not so long ago, the only time we ate romaine lettuce was in a Caesar salad or chopped in a mix of lettuces. In the early 2000s, romaine—also known as kos or cos lettuce—suddenly became the go-to vegetable at the summer grill. When grilled, it has an interesting mix of textures, as the core stays crisp and sweet while the leaves get soft and smoky. Malt vinegar highlights this mix, but you can also use balsamic or sherry vinegar. The cheese garnish can be almost any cheese you like; a crumbled blue or creamy goat works very well.

Preheat and oil the grill. (Alternatively, preheat the oven to 450°F and lightly coat a large rimmed baking sheet with olive oil.)

Using a sharp knife, cut each romaine heart in half lengthwise, keeping the core intact.

Generously coat the entire lettuce with olive oil and season with salt and cracked black pepper. Place on the preheated grill, cut side down, and grill for about 4 minutes, turning once, or until slightly wilted and charred around the edges. (Alternatively, place cut sides down on the prepared baking sheet and roast in the oven, turning once, for about 7 minutes.)

Using tongs, transfer the romaine halves to a serving platter, cut side up. Drizzle with the vinegar and sprinkle the crumbled cheese over the top. Serve hot, warm, or at room temperature.

Vella Cheese

I'm a bit spoiled as the Vella Cheese Company is right in Sonoma: We all love their renowned Dry Jack cheese, a very firm wheel of golden cheese that is the perfect mix of nutty, salty, and slightly sweet. Vella is a family-owned company founded in 1931 by Tom Vella, long before the current interest in cheese making. His son, Ignacio, is a legend in the world of artisanal cheeses, having mentored many of the young, award-winning cheesemakers in America today. Although California was the leader in the artisanal cheese movement, there are now superb handmade cheeses being created all across the country.

CHAPTER 4

PASTA AND GRAINS

Pasta has changed drastically over the years. Gnocchi, ravioli, all shapes of dried pasta, pasta machines, great Parmesan cheese, olives, and olive oils are now in kitchens all across America, along with heirloom grains and rice and noodles from all over Asia. As with all ingredients, the better the quality, the better the dish. Although artisanal pastas are slightly more expensive, they are well worth the extra cost and in the end they taste much better.

PASTA BEURRE BLANC

Serves 6

1 pound imported Italian
fusilli, penne, or any shape
you prefer

3 tablespoons unsalted butter

½ cup grated Pecorino Romano
or Parmesan cheese, plus
more for serving

Salt and pepper

This is about as simple a pasta as you can prepare—it can be thrown together in a few minutes and is, without a doubt, one of the boys' favorite quick meals. If you want to fancy it up, toss in some chopped basil, parsley, or chives. Otherwise, just put the whole shebang in a large warm pasta bowl with some extra cheese on the side. It will be gone before you sit down.

Bring a large pot of salted water to boil over high heat. The water should be as salty as the sea. When rapidly boiling, add the pasta and cook according to package directions, usually between 12 and 15 minutes.

Remove from the heat and drain well, reserving 1 cup of the pasta cooking water.

Return the reserved cooking water to the pot and place over high heat. Add the butter and bring to a boil. Add the pasta along with the cheese and toss to coat with the "sauce." Season with salt and pepper and serve with grated cheese on the side.

TAGLIATELLE WITH BROCCOLI PESTO

Serves 6

1 pound imported Italian tagliatelle
or other dry pasta of choice

Broccoli Pesto (recipe follows)

Pepper

About ¾ cup grated
Parmesan cheese

Although pesto is usually made with cheese, this one has none.
Nor does it have the usual pine nuts, as I can't resist using flavorful
California walnuts instead. Nor is the traditional fresh basil the base;
it has the surprise of blanched broccoli as the green. All in all, a very
different pesto, but nonetheless a delicious one.

Bring a large pot of salted water to a boil over high heat. The water
should be as salty as the sea. When rapidly boiling, add the pasta and
cook according to package directions, usually between 12 and
15 minutes.

Drain well, reserving about ½ cup of the pasta cooking water.

Return the pasta to the cooking pot and add about three-fourths of
the pesto along with the reserved cooking water. Season with pepper
and toss to coat.

Using tongs, transfer an equal portion to each of 6 pasta bowls.
Place a dollop of the remaining pesto on top of each and sprinkle with
a generous serving of cheese. Serve immediately.

BROCCOLI PESTO

Makes about 2 cups

1 bunch broccoli

3 cloves garlic, chopped

1 cup chopped toasted walnuts

1 cup fresh flat-leaf parsley leaves

2 tablespoons fresh mint leaves

⅓ cup extra-virgin olive oil

Trim the tough end stalks and any leaves from the broccoli and cut
into large pieces.

Bring a large pot of water to a boil over high heat. When boiling,
add the broccoli and cook for about 3 minutes or just until slightly
cooked, but still bright green. Drain well in a fine mesh sieve.

Place the drained broccoli under cold running water to stop the
cooking. Drain well, then place on a double layer of paper towels to
drain completely. You might also want to use paper towels to pat it
dry as you don't want the pesto to be waterlogged.

When the broccoli is dry, place it in the bowl of a food processor
fitted with the metal blade. Add the garlic, walnuts, parsley, and mint
and process, using quick on-and-off turns, for about 3 minutes or
until finely chopped. With the motor running, slowly add the olive oil,
processing until just incorporated. Do not puree.

Scrape the mixture into a clean container. Use immediately or store,
covered and refrigerated, for up to 3 days, or freeze for up to 3 months.
If refrigerated or frozen, bring to room temperature before using.

FRESH PASTA WITH
DOUBLE TOMATO SAUCE

Serves 6

½ cup extra-virgin olive oil such
as Zamparelli (see Note)

1½ pounds heirloom cherry
tomatoes, cut in half lengthwise

½ cup finely chopped
sun-dried tomatoes
(see Sun-Dried Tomatoes, page 80)

¼ cup capers packed in salt,
rinsed and dried

3 tablespoons white
balsamic vinegar

Salt and cracked black pepper

Pasta Dough (recipe follows),
cut for spaghetti or fettuccine

1 cup coarsely chopped fresh basil

1 cup grated Asiago cheese

I've given you a recipe to make your own fresh pasta, but if you want to take a shortcut, there are lots of wonderful commercially prepared fresh pastas that would work very well in this recipe. In New York City there are a number of extraordinary Italian markets ranging from the hyper-store Eataly to mom-and-pop stores on Arthur Avenue in the Bronx, and in my travels across the country I've seen fresh pasta in supermarkets—so if you are not in the mood to spend an afternoon in the kitchen, you can still enjoy this dish.

Bring a large pot of salted water to a boil over high heat. The water should be as salty as the sea.

Warm the olive oil in a large frying pan over medium heat. Do not allow it to get very hot. Add the cherry tomatoes, sun-dried tomatoes, and capers and cook just until heated through. Remove from the heat and add the vinegar, stirring to blend. Season with salt and cracked pepper and keep warm.

When the water is rapidly boiling, add the pasta and cook until al dente, about 2 minutes. Drain well.

Add the pasta to the tomato mixture, then add the basil and toss gently to combine.

Using tongs, transfer an equal portion to each of 6 pasta bowls. Generously sprinkle cheese over the tops and serve.

Note: I first tasted Zamparelli Oro extra-virgin olive oil at Eataly in New York City and became an instant convert. It is a beautiful yellow-green in color, slightly peppery, and very grassy in flavor with an almost flowery aroma. I use it on grilled vegetables, tomato pasta dishes, and as a garnish on soups. Although I don't usually cook with it, in this recipe I just warm it a bit as the warmth seems to cause it to exhibit some tomato-like flavor. You can, of course, use any high-quality grassy extra-virgin olive oil in its place.

Continued

Sun-Dried Tomatoes

If you would like to make your own sun-dried tomatoes, they take almost no work, but they do take time. Preheat the oven to 175°F. Place wire racks (like those you use to cool cookies) on each of 2 rimmed baking sheets. Start with about 3 pounds organic Roma tomatoes. Slice them in half lengthwise and scoop out and discard the seeds and membranes. Season with salt, pepper, and dried oregano. Place the tomatoes, cut side down, in a single layer on the racks. Transfer to the preheated oven and dry for at least 12 hours. This method will yield tomatoes that are semi-dry. If you want them to be truly sun-dried, after oven-drying, place them in the sunniest spot you can find for as long as it takes to create intensely flavored, shriveled tomatoes. Unfortunately, you will have to bring the tomatoes indoors at night so that nighttime moisture does not impede the drying process. About 3 pounds (about 30 Roma) ripe tomatoes will yield only about 1 cup of completely sun-dried; substantially more in weight for semi-dried. You can also dry tomatoes in a dehydrator according to the manufacturer's directions; they will be dried, but not sun-dried. Store the dried tomatoes in an airtight container at room temperature. You can also cover them with extra-virgin olive oil. For more savory tomatoes, when covered in olive oil add a tablespoon or so of fresh rosemary or basil along with a couple of roasted garlic cloves.

PASTA DOUGH

1 pound 00 flour plus more for flouring the board or your hands (see Note, page 49)

1 teaspoon salt

4 large eggs, at room temperature

1 tablespoon olive oil

Semolina flour for dusting

Makes about 1½ pounds

Set up a heavy-duty stand mixer with the pasta rolling attachment. To make spaghetti or fettuccine, you will also need the pasta cutting attachment or, if you don't mind uneven strands, you can attempt cutting the pasta into strings by hand.

Place flour in a small bowl and keep close at hand as you might need to flour the work surface, the finished dough, or your hands to keep the dough from sticking.

Combine the remaining 1 pound of flour and salt on a clean work surface, slightly mounding it in the center. Make a well in the center and place the eggs and oil in the well. Using your fingertips, loosen the eggs and incorporate a bit of the oil into them. Then slowly pull the flour into the well, working from the outside in, moving in a circular motion. Continue mixing in this motion until all of the flour has been incorporated into the dough and it easily pulls into a ball.

Lightly dust a clean work surface with flour and begin kneading the dough by flattening it out and folding it over and over until smooth and elastic. This can take up to 15 minutes.

Divide the dough into 2 or 3 pieces. Immediately wrap each piece in plastic wrap and set aside to rest for 1 hour.

When ready to roll out, unwrap one piece of dough and push it into a long rectangle. Begin rolling it through the pasta machine on the widest setting. Roll at least 3 times, stretching the dough with your hands as it comes out of the roller. Then begin reducing the settings and pushing the dough through each one 2 to 3 times. Roll until you are on the thinnest setting and the dough is about ⅛ inch thick. Continue making pasta until all of the dough has been rolled.

At this point, the dough is ready to be used as is or cut into shapes. If cutting into shapes, place the particular attachment on your mixer and follow the manufacturer's directions for the shape you desire. I like either spaghetti or fettuccine for the above recipe.

If not using immediately, freshly made pasta should be dusted with semolina flour to keep it from sticking. If using large pieces or making ravioli, place the sheets on a semolina-dusted baking sheet and cover with a clean kitchen towel until ready to cook or fill. When making noodles, drape the noodles over a pasta drying rack or the back of a kitchen chair until ready to cook.

Fresh pasta is cooked in boiling salted water just as dried, except that it cooks very quickly, usually within 1 to 3 minutes depending upon the shape; fettuccine should take about 2 minutes. Since it is extremely tender, it should be carefully drained and used immediately.

GREEN TEA SOBA NOODLES WITH TUNA

Serves 6

¼ cup rice wine vinegar

¼ cup soy sauce

1 tablespoon lemon juice

1 tablespoon mirin

1 teaspoon minced garlic

1 teaspoon grated fresh ginger

¾ cup avocado oil

2 tablespoons toasted sesame oil

2 tablespoons chopped scallions

2 teaspoons toasted sesame seeds

12 ounces green tea soba noodles (see Note)

2 ribs celery, trimmed and shaved crosswise

1 large carrot, peeled and shaved crosswise

1½ pounds ahi tuna, cut into ½-inch dice

When the boys were small, they enjoyed a soba noodle dish much like this one at Aureole in New York. They loved the noodles and the raw tuna and went on to become sushi connoisseurs. Consequently, I make some version of soba and raw fish at least once a week.

Bring a large pot of salted water to boil over high heat. The water should be as salty as the sea.

Combine the rice wine vinegar, soy sauce, lemon juice, and mirin in a small mixing bowl and whisk to blend well. Add the garlic and ginger and stir to combine. Begin whisking in the avocado oil and, when blended, whisk in the sesame oil. Transfer to a serving bowl and stir in the scallions and sesame seeds. Set the dressing aside.

Add the soba noodles to the boiling water, stirring to loosen them. Return the water to a strong boil, lower the heat, and continue to cook for about 3 minutes or until the noodles are tender. Drain well. Rinse in cold water and place in a colander and drain completely.

Place the soba noodles on a serving platter. Add the celery and carrot, toss to combine, and top with the diced tuna. Serve the sesame dressing on the side.

Note: Soba noodles are thin Japanese buckwheat noodles that can be served either cold with a dashi-flavored dipping sauce (called *soba tsuyu*) or in a hot dashi broth as for a noodle soup. For cold noodles, the diner picks them up with chopsticks, swirls them around in the sauce, and slurps them up. Throughout Japan they are served as fast food on the street and at railway stations as well as in fine dining and soba specialty restaurants. There are a number of different kinds of soba noodles; noodles flavored with green tea powder are known as *cha soba*. They are available at Japanese markets, specialty food stores, many supermarkets, and online.

WILD-MUSHROOM BARLEY **RISOTTO**

Serves 6

1 tablespoon olive oil

6 ounces pancetta, finely diced

2 leeks (white parts only), well washed and cut crosswise into thin slices

½ pound wild mushrooms, trimmed, cleaned, and sliced

2 cups pearl barley

4 sprigs fresh thyme

2 cloves garlic, minced

Salt and pepper

¾ cup red wine

6 cups chicken stock or canned nonfat, low-sodium chicken broth

½ cup grated Parmesan, plus more for serving

1 tablespoon chopped fresh flat-leaf parsley

Rather than always using the traditional rice for risotto, I like to mix it up with other grains. This is probably something I wouldn't have thought of early in my career, but with the recent emphasis on healthy eating, I find that I am trying more grains and beans than I would have once thought possible. If you are not a grain fan, you can make this using arborio, carnaroli, or any medium-grain white rice.

Heat the oil in a large, heavy-bottomed saucepan over medium heat. Add the pancetta and cook, stirring frequently, for about 7 minutes or just until the meat begins to brown. Add the leeks and mushrooms and continue to cook, stirring frequently, for another 5 minutes or until the leeks and mushrooms begin to color. Stir in the barley along with the thyme and garlic and cook for 2 minutes. Season with salt and pepper.

Add the wine and cook for about 5 minutes or just until the wine has been absorbed by the barley. It will darken in color. Stir in half of the stock, raise the heat, and bring to a boil. Immediately lower the heat, cover, and cook at a bare simmer for about 12 minutes or until all of the liquid has been absorbed. Uncover and stir in the remaining stock. Again, cover and continue to cook for another 12 minutes or until the barley is tender and all of the liquid has been absorbed.

Stir in the cheese along with the parsley. Spoon equal portions of the "risotto" into 6 shallow pasta bowls, sprinkle with more cheese, and serve.

CHAPTER 5

MEAT AND BIRDS

I love cooking meat—from pork to lamb, beef to wild game, and all types of birds—there's such a richness of flavor and so much you can do. I particularly support the recent trend of bringing heritage animal breeds raised on small family farms to the dinner table. These breeds have evolved over centuries through their ability to thrive in a specific environment and have been continually bred for the flavor and texture of their meat. As the owner of steak houses, I know that diners like nothing better than a char-grilled steak, some tempting side dishes, and a beautiful bottle of Bordeaux wine. Here I give you some meat- and poultry-centric recipes that embrace America's love of meat at the center of the plate.

WORKING THE GRILL

I THINK THAT the main reason I love to grill is that I come from a long line of meat-eaters—and what better way to enjoy a great piece of meat than slightly charred, hot and juicy right off of the grill? And to the grill masters in my family, grilling is not work, it is an art to be practiced standing around the barbecue with friends and a glass of vintage wine. Obviously it is not an everyday occurrence, but it is one that my family enjoys so much that we tend to grill more frequently than most. The aroma of the smoke itself signals everyone to get ready for a relaxed good time. Once we get the meat or fish on the grill, company gathers round, eagerly awaiting the first chance for a sample. I've also embraced my stovetop grill pan, which, though it doesn't offer the wood-smoked char that the outdoor grill gives, marks the meat nicely and makes me feel as though I've been manning an open fire.

Since my family now lives part-time in California where I can grill all year long, I have expanded my grilling repertoire from speidies (see page 90) to include almost anything you can imagine. It is such a leisurely way to feed a crowd and, by using ingredients beyond the everyday hamburgers and grilled chicken, create an elegant meal with ease. The boys love to help, which makes getting dinner on the table a family affair.

Originally I just thought of the grill as a stove to cook protein, but since we have so many marvelous ingredients and cuisines from which to choose, I now hang loose and experiment. While the usual picnic fare still works for me, I can easily put all types of vegetables, a whole fish (such as sturgeon), quail, venison, or lobster on the fire. Grilling sets the mood with the fire glowing, aromatic smoke rising, and the air fragrant with the charring—all you need is some good friends (but I must say strangers quickly become friends in this setting) and some terrific wine to complete the scene.

I am lucky enough to have a wood-fired oven as well as a charcoal grill, so I can create amazing meals outdoors. When grilling, I often experiment with different types of hardwood chips, which will flavor the grilled item in new and interesting ways. Whatever style grill you use—charcoal or gas—get to know it well so that you are comfortable with its quirks. There is nothing more unpleasant than having a crowd waiting for the grill master to get the show on the road.

HERE ARE A FEW GRILLING TIPS THAT I'VE LEARNED ALONG THE WAY:

1. Don't rely on the old standards. Even picky eaters will enjoy something new off the grill.

2. Rather than meat every time, try grilling vegetables, fish, and shellfish. It's quick, easy, and absolutely delicious. One of my favorite grills was of a large, wild sturgeon, simply because so few of our guests had ever tasted this firm, delicately flavored fish except in its smoked form. Before grilling, you can marinate fresh fish or season it with almost any combination of herbs and spices, but I prefer it unadorned. When pristine, there is nothing more delicious than wild fish, grilled with just a hint of salt and pepper and drizzled with a bit of fresh lemon and extra-virgin olive oil at the table.

3. In place of the standard hot dog, try different types of sausages. There are now well-seasoned chicken and turkey sausages to be had in the supermarket, and ethnic sausages are available online or through specialty butchers. Try them all for the variety they offer.

4. In place of meat, marinate large, meaty portobello mushrooms in speidie sauce or any other flavorful marinade for about 30 minutes before grilling. Serve them on a toasted bun with spicy greens and roasted red peppers.

5. At cocktail time, grill up an array of shellfish: Lobster claws, heads-on shrimp, clams, and oysters are but a tiny taste of the shellfish platters I might serve with chilled white wine, such as our Sonoma local favorites, a Rochioli or Mauritson sauvignon blanc or champagne. Warm, straight-from-the-grill oysters with a savory butter, refreshing salsa, or mignonette would be the perfect beginning to an evening of grilling with family and friends.

6. Game birds wrapped in pancetta, or other slightly spicy hams, and thick, succulent chops send up enticing aromas.

CHARLIE'S SPEIDIE
MARINADE

Makes about 3 cups, enough for 5 pounds meat or poultry

2 cups dry white wine

¼ cup sherry wine vinegar

¼ cup canola oil

½ cup finely minced shallots

1 tablespoon minced garlic

1 tablespoon minced fresh
flat-leaf parsley

2 bay leaves, crumbled

¼ teaspoon dried thyme

¼ teaspoon dried oregano

Salt and pepper

In upstate New York where I grew up, summertime is speidie time. Speidies are beef or chicken kabobs marinated in a locally produced speidie sauce and cooked on the grill. Almost nobody makes their own sauce; it is purchased by the case to take the barbecue master through the entire summer's grilling. This is not a complicated sauce, but a slightly acidic, simple marinade that works as an accent to all types of grilled meats, and I happily share it with you.

Combine all of the ingredients in a nonreactive container. Cover and allow flavors to blend for at least 1 hour before using. May be stored, refrigerated, for up to 1 week. The marinade can be used for any meat, poultry, or game.

FLORENTINE ROASTED **STRIP LOIN,** NEW POTATOES, AND PARMESAN ASPARAGUS

Serves 6

1 (5-pound) beef strip loin, fat trimmed to about ¼ inch

1 cup extra-virgin olive oil

⅓ cup chopped fresh rosemary

¼ cup minced garlic

1½ pounds small Yukon gold new potatoes, about 1½-inch around

10 cloves garlic, peeled

Sea salt and cracked black pepper

Parmesan Asparagus (recipe follows)

When we were all in Italy, we were served the most extraordinary *bistecca alla fiorentina* (beefsteak in the style of Florence). The T-bone steak was about 4 inches thick, served very rare, and carved at the table. Traditionally, the meat comes from the famous Chianina or Maremmana breeds that have roamed the fields of Tuscany for hundreds of years. The steak is grilled, simply seasoned with salt and pepper, over a wood fire. We had to try our hand at the grill as soon as we got home; the boys insisted that this was the best steak they had ever eaten. Rather than test the waters with a T-bone, I roasted a strip loin in my wood-fired oven. It has now become a Palmer specialty, especially when served with crisp golden potatoes and asparagus.

I usually pair a Chianti with the steak. I use it as a geography lesson for the boys. That is, pair your dish with a wine from its region; the flavors will almost always marry well.

Place the strip loin in a large baking dish. Combine ¾ cup of the olive oil with about ¼ cup of the rosemary and all of the minced garlic and pour it over the meat. Use your fingertips to massage the seasoned oil into the meat. Cover with plastic wrap and set aside to marinate for at least 2 hours or up to 8 hours. If marinating longer than 2 hours, refrigerate and then bring to room temperate about an hour before you are ready to cook.

Combine the potatoes with the remaining ¼ cup olive oil and the remaining rosemary along with the garlic cloves in a shallow ceramic baking dish large enough to hold them in a single layer. Season with sea salt and cracked black pepper and set aside.

If you are lucky enough to have one, build a hot fire in a wood-fired oven (noting that a wood-fired oven ranges from 450°F to 600°F). Alternatively, preheat the oven to 450°F and place the roasting pan in the oven to get it very hot; or preheat a charcoal grill to high.

Place the seasoned roast, fat side up, in a heavy-duty roasting pan. Transfer to the wood-fired or traditional oven. (Alternatively, transfer the meat to the preheated, very hot grill and cover the grill.) Place the pan holding the potatoes in the oven along with the roast. (If your oven is large enough or you have 2 ovens, the asparagus can go in now as well.)

Roast (or grill) the steak for about 10 minutes, turning occasionally, to brown all sides. Then continue to roast (or grill) for about 20 minutes or until an instant-read thermometer inserted into the thickest part reads 125°F for medium-rare or 140°F for medium.

Roast the potatoes, shaking the pan occasionally to ensure even browning, for about 35 minutes or until cooked through, golden, and crisp. If grilling the steak, roast the potatoes in the preheated oven.

Place the loin on a carving board with a channel for catching juices. Tent lightly with aluminum foil and let rest for 10 minutes.

Using a sharp knife, cut the meat crosswise into thick slices. Serve on the carving board with the potatoes scattered around and the asparagus on the side.

PARMESAN ASPARAGUS

Serves 6 to 8

1½ pounds asparagus, tough ends snapped off

¼ cup extra-virgin olive oil

Grated zest of 1 lemon

Salt and pepper

Block of Parmesan cheese for shaving

Preheat the oven to 450°F.

If the asparagus is large, you might want to peel off the lower skin as it can be tough. This is not necessary for small or medium spears.

Fill a bowl large enough to hold the asparagus with iced water. Set aside.

Bring a large pot of salted water to boil over high heat. Add the asparagus and cook for about 1 minute or just until bright green and still crisp. Drain. Immediately place in the iced water to stop the cooking. As soon as the asparagus cools, drain well and pat dry.

Place the dried asparagus on a rimmed baking sheet. Add the olive oil, lemon zest, and salt and pepper, tossing to coat evenly.

Roast, turning occasionally, for about 20 minutes or until nicely charred and tender.

Transfer to a serving platter. While still very hot, shave Parmesan cheese over the top. Serve immediately.

GRILLED FLANK STEAK WITH POMEGRANATE SALAD

Serves 6

¼ cup extra-virgin olive oil

¼ cup balsamic vinegar

1 tablespoon pomegranate molasses (see Note)

1 tablespoon minced garlic

2 teaspoons fresh thyme leaves

1 tablespoon paprika

2 (1½- to 2-pound) flank steaks

Salt and pepper

1 pound heirloom cherry tomatoes, cut in half lengthwise

1 small head chicory, well washed, tough ends removed, chopped

4 ounces chopped toasted walnuts

¼ cup pomegranate seeds

Pomegranate Dressing (recipe follows)

Pomegranates are another fruit that I didn't know much about when I started cooking, but they sure are well known now, due especially to their antioxidant qualities. I see the seeds in the produce section of supermarkets, and the juice is everywhere and in everything. The tart and sweet flavors that explode in your mouth make the fruit a wonderful accent to beef or any rich meat.

Combine the olive oil, vinegar, pomegranate molasses, garlic, and thyme in a small mixing bowl, whisking to blend well.

Working with one at a time and using your fingertips, massage the paprika into the steaks. Rub the pomegranate marinade into both sides of the steaks, making sure that it covers the meat. Transfer to a glass baking dish, wrap with plastic wrap, and set aside to marinate for 1 hour.

Preheat and oil the grill.

Remove the steaks from the baking dish and season with salt and pepper. Place on the hot grill. Grill, turning occasionally, for about 12 minutes for rare or 15 minutes for medium. Place the steaks on a carving board with a channel for catching juices and let rest for 5 minutes.

While the steaks are grilling, make the salad.

Combine the tomatoes with the chicory, walnuts, and pomegranate seeds in a medium mixing bowl. Add just enough dressing to lightly coat.

Using a sharp carving knife, cut the steaks on the bias into thin strips and transfer to a serving platter in slightly overlapping slices. Drizzle the juices over the top and place the salad around and on the steak on the platter. Serve immediately.

Note: Pomegranate molasses is a necessary ingredient in many Middle Eastern dishes. The tart and sweet syrup, made from cooking pomegranate juice with sugar, is available at Middle Eastern markets, specialty food stores, some supermarkets, and online. It is quite sticky and thick—somewhat more so than ketchup—with a glorious garnet color. It is terrific in barbecue sauces.

Continued

2 tablespoons pomegranate molasses

1 tablespoon orange juice

½ teaspoon minced garlic

¼ cup walnut oil

Salt and pepper

POMEGRANATE DRESSING

Makes about ½ cup

Combine the molasses with the orange juice and garlic in a small mixing bowl. Add the walnut oil and whisk to combine. Season with salt and pepper.

Use as directed or store, covered and refrigerated, for up to 3 days. Bring to room temperature before using.

Wine Pairing: I love cabernet grapes. These rich, sought-after wines are made from the world's great food grapes. Some of my California favorites are Silver Oak and Dominus, but you'll also find the great Château Margaux at the top of my list.

SLOW-BRAISED **BEEF CHEEKS** AND MELTED ONIONS

Serves 6

8 large beef cheeks or
4 pounds beef chuck,
cut into large cubes

About 1 cup all-purpose flour

Salt and pepper

¼ cup canola oil

¼ cup (½ stick) unsalted butter

6 onions, cut crosswise
into thin slices

2 tablespoons balsamic vinegar

1 tablespoon minced garlic

5 cups beef stock or canned nonfat,
low-sodium beef broth

1 cup dry red wine

2 tablespoons Worcestershire
sauce

4 sprigs fresh thyme

3 bay leaves

2 tablespoons chopped fresh
flat-leaf parsley

Sautéed Swiss Chard with Feta
(page 197)

The boys discovered beef cheeks on the menu at my flagship restaurant, Aureole, in New York City. They decided that they liked them far better than the short ribs I'd been making at home. I try to make it an all-in-one dish, with the onions making a sweet, savory sauce and the chard rounding out the meal. If you can't find beef cheeks, beef stew meat will do just fine; and if you are still a short rib fan, this recipe works very well with them. I generally serve the cheeks with Sautéed Swiss Chard with Feta (page 197).

Preheat the oven to 300°F.

Place the beef in a large bowl. Add the flour and season with salt and pepper, tossing to coat well. Remove the beef cubes from the seasoned flour, shaking off any excess.

Heat the oil in a Dutch oven with a lid over medium heat. Add the beef, a few pieces at a time, and sear, turning occasionally, until nicely browned on all sides. As seared, transfer to a plate.

When all of the beef has been seared, wipe any fat from the pan, return to medium heat, and add the butter. When the butter has melted, add the onions and cook, stirring occasionally, for 10 minutes or until beginning to color. Stir in the vinegar and garlic and continue to cook, stirring occasionally, for another 10 minutes or just until the onions begin to caramelize.

Add the stock, wine, and Worcestershire sauce, stirring to blend. Add the seared beef along with the thyme and bay leaves. The liquid should just barely cover the meat. Cover the pan and bake, occasionally turning the meat, for about 3 hours or until the beef is very, very tender.

Using a slotted spoon, transfer the meat to a warm serving platter. Tent lightly with aluminum foil and keep warm.

Place the Dutch oven over high heat and bring the remaining liquid to a boil. Boil for about 10 minutes or until the liquid and onions are reduced to a sauce-like consistency. Taste and, if necessary, season with salt and pepper.

Pour some of the melted onion sauce over the meat and pass the remainder on the side. Sprinkle with parsley and serve with the Swiss chard.

Note: Beef cheeks are exactly that, the cheek muscles of a cow. They have only recently been found on restaurant menus, but have been used by thrifty home cooks for generations. The meat is extremely lean and therefore quite tough, so it takes a long, slow braise to tenderize it.

Wine Pairing: Rafanelli merlot is a superbly balanced red that I love to serve with beef cheeks or short ribs, no matter the vegetable accompanying them. It is rich, but yet has great acidity to cut through the fattiness of the meat.

BURGERS
THREE WAYS

When I make burgers at a barbecue, I like to offer a variety. Serving just beef burgers doesn't always work anymore, because there's always one or two people who don't eat red meat. So try introducing new versions to your outdoor entertaining and spice it up a bit. For every pound of ground meat—beef, turkey, chicken, venison, or a mix—add ½ cup minced red onion along with 2 tablespoons minced fresh herbs (or minced chile peppers to taste) and chopped cilantro (or 1 tablespoon roasted garlic puree, see page 28). Or try ½ cup ketchup, 2 tablespoons dark beer, 1 tablespoon Dijon mustard, 1 tablespoon minced onion, and ¾ cup fresh bread crumbs. Or, finally, form a burger around a 1-inch cube of cheddar, Jack, Brie, or any other cheese you like. Any of these will add some spice to tradition.

TRADITIONAL BURGERS

Serves 6

1½ pounds coarsely ground beef sirloin

1½ pounds ground beef chuck

¼ cup finely minced onion

2 tablespoons ice water (see Note)

Salt and pepper

Olive oil to brush on patties

6 thick (¼-inch) slices cheese (any kind you like; I generally stick with cheddar), optional

6 large brioche buns, split and toasted

Condiments of choice: mustard (yellow or Dijon), ketchup, pickle relish, hot chile relish, mayonnaise, aioli, salsa, sliced tomato, sliced sweet or dill pickles, grilled or raw onions, lettuce leaves

Place the sirloin and chuck in a medium bowl. Add the onion and ice water and season with salt and pepper. Using your hands, gently mix to blend well.

Form the mixture into 6 equal mounds (so they cook evenly) and shape each into a patty. Using a pastry brush, generously coat the outside of the patties with oil.

Preheat and oil the grill or preheat a nonstick stovetop grill pan over medium-high heat. When very hot, add the patties and grill for about 5 minutes or until crusty and nicely browned on the bottom. Turn and grill the remaining side for about 4 minutes or until brown and crusty and the burger is medium-rare—unless you want it well done, which will require about 4 additional minutes of cooking. If you want to make cheeseburgers, place a slice of cheese on the burgers when you turn them.

Place a burger on each bun. Serve with any condiments you like.

Note: I always add a bit of ice water to my burgers as it helps distribute the seasonings evenly as well as ensures that the burgers stay moist and juicy.

PORTOBELLO BURGERS

Serves 6

6 large portobello mushrooms, stems removed

½ cup balsamic vinegar

½ cup extra-virgin olive oil

1 tablespoon chopped fresh flat-leaf parsley

2 teaspoons chopped fresh basil leaves

Salt and pepper

6 thick slices provolone cheese

6 ciabatta rolls, split and toasted

6 roasted red bell pepper halves

4 ounces arugula, tough stems removed

Using damp paper towels, wipe the mushrooms clean. Place in a shallow baking dish, gill side up.

Combine the vinegar, oil, parsley, and basil in a small mixing bowl, whisking to blend. Pour the vinegar mixture over the mushrooms. Set aside to marinate for at least 30 minutes or up to 3 hours.

Preheat and oil the grill or preheat a nonstick stovetop grill pan over medium-high heat. Remove the mushrooms from the marinade and place them on the grill, gill side up. Season with salt and pepper and grill, turning once, for about 5 minutes or until charred and nicely browned on the bottom. Turn and place a slice of cheese on each mushroom and grill the remaining side for about 4 minutes or until the mushrooms are cooked through and the cheese has melted.

Place a mushroom on each roll, top with equal portions of the bell peppers and arugula, and serve.

Damn Good Burger

Should you be in Costa Mesa, California, stop in at DG Burger, my fast casual restaurant featuring my signature Damn Good Burger: Black Angus beef topped with cabbage, tomato, red onion, and my DG sauce, served on a semolina potato bun. We also feature a vegetable burger and a chicken sandwich, along with the best fries you'll ever taste and old-fashioned malted milk shakes.

CHICKEN OR TURKEY BURGERS

Serves 6

2 pounds ground chicken or turkey

1 large egg, at room temperature

1 serrano or other hot green chile (or to taste), stemmed, seeded, and minced

¼ cup minced red bell pepper

2 tablespoons minced shallot

1 teaspoon minced garlic

1 teaspoon ground chile powder (not seasoned chili powder)

¼ teaspoon ground cumin

Salt and pepper

Olive oil to brush on patties

6 large brioche buns, split and toasted

Guacamole (recipe follows)

Combine the chicken or turkey with the egg, using your hands to blend. Add the chile, bell pepper, shallot, garlic, chile powder, and cumin. Again, using your hands, mix well to blend. Season with salt and pepper.

Preheat and oil the grill, or preheat a nonstick stovetop grill pan over medium-high heat.

Form the mixture into 6 equal mounds (so they cook evenly) and shape each into a patty. Using a pastry brush, generously coat the outside of each with oil.

Place the burgers on the grill and grill for 6 minutes. Turn and grill for another 5 minutes for well done.

Place a burger on each bun, top with guacamole, and serve.

GUACAMOLE

Makes about 2 cups

2 large avocados, pitted, peeled, and mashed

Juice of 1 lime

⅓ cup chopped, seeded, and peeled tomato

2 tablespoons minced red onion

2 tablespoons chopped cilantro

1 teaspoon minced and seeded serrano chile, optional

Salt

Combine the avocado with the lime juice, tomato, onion, cilantro, and chile. Season with salt and serve.

STUFFED
CABBAGE ROLLS

Serves 6 to 8

24 large green cabbage leaves

1½ cups minced onion

4 cups tomato puree

2 cups vegetable stock or canned nonfat, low-sodium vegetable broth

¼ cup dark loosely packed brown sugar

3 tablespoons red wine vinegar

½ pound ground beef

½ pound ground pork

2 cups cooked long grain rice

1 large egg

1 tablespoon tomato paste

2 tablespoons finely chopped fresh parsley leaves

2 tablespoons minced celery

1 teaspoon minced garlic

Salt and pepper

1 cup sour cream

This very hearty dish has its origin in Eastern Europe, but I think many old-time home cooks have a version that they have made their own. Although some cooks fill the rolls and then cook them in a meat-based broth, I like a rich tomato–sour cream sauce. You can use either regular green cabbage or Savoy. You can also use this recipe to make stuffed squash, bell peppers, or eggplant, replacing the cabbage leaves with the pertinent vegetable.

Bring a large pot of lightly salted water to a boil over high heat. Fill a large bowl with ice water.

Working with one or two leaves at a time, place the cabbage in the boiling water for about 1 minute or until just pliable. Immediately dip the softened leaf into the ice water to stop the cooking. Drain well and pat dry. If the main vein at the core end of a leaf is very thick, trim it down slightly with a paring knife, but don't trim too much as the leaf has to be sturdy enough to hold the filling. Set the leaves aside.

Preheat the oven to 375°F.

Combine 1 cup of the onion with the tomato puree, stock, brown sugar, and vinegar in a large Dutch oven. Place over medium heat and bring the sauce to a low simmer.

Combine the remaining ½ cup onion with the ground beef, ground pork, and rice in a large mixing bowl. Add the egg, tomato paste, parsley, celery, and garlic and season with salt and pepper. Using your hands, gently bring the mixture together, without mashing the rice, until completely blended.

Working with one cabbage leaf at a time, place about ¼ cup of the meat mixture near the core end of a leaf. Fold in each side of the leaf to almost cover the filling. Fold the stem end over and continue to roll to completely enclose the filling. Using a toothpick, close the roll together at the end by weaving the toothpick in and out to hold the leaf tightly around the filling. Carefully place the cabbage roll in the simmering sauce. Repeat to make all the cabbage rolls.

Cover the Dutch oven and bake the rolls for about 45 minutes or until the meat stuffing is cooked through and the leaves are very tender.

Using a slotted spoon, transfer the cabbage rolls to a large serving platter with raised sides.

Place the Dutch oven over medium-low heat and whisk the sour cream into the cooking juices. Do not let the mixture come to a boil. Taste and, if necessary, season with salt and pepper. Pour the sauce over the rolls on the platter and serve with any extra sauce on the side.

Serve immediately or allow to cool and store, covered and refrigerated, for up to 3 days, or freeze for up to 3 months. Reheat before serving.

PAN-SEARED
VEAL CHOPS WITH
WILD MUSHROOM GRATINS

Serves 6

¼ cup extra-virgin olive oil

2 tablespoons minced garlic
(or to taste)

2 tablespoons chopped fresh
rosemary

1 tablespoon fresh thyme leaves

6 thick (at least 1-inch) rib veal
chops

1 tablespoon canola oil

1 tablespoon unsalted butter

2 shallots, minced

2 pounds wild mushrooms,
cleaned, stems removed, sliced

2 teaspoons fines herbes

Salt and pepper

3 tablespoons all-purpose flour

1 cup heavy cream

Freshly grated nutmeg to taste

1 cup grated Gruyère cheese

2 tablespoons minced fresh chives

Simple, but yet restaurant-style. This would be a great meal to serve at a dinner party as the last-minute cooking is less than 15 minutes. If you don't feel like making the gratins, this is still a great way to cook veal or lamb chops. Just make sure that you don't overcook them, as both veal and lamb chops are best when they are pink and juicy. Of course, the veal chop would not be complete without a glass of Châteauneuf-du-Pape to accompany.

Combine the olive oil with the garlic, rosemary, and thyme in a baking dish large enough to hold the chops. Place the chops in the baking dish and turn to coat both sides with the oil mixture. Set aside to marinate, turning occasionally, for 30 minutes.

Preheat the oven to 450°F. Lightly butter six 6-ounce ramekins.

Heat the canola oil and butter in a large sauté pan over medium heat. Add the shallots and cook, stirring occasionally, for about 3 minutes or until just translucent. Add the mushrooms and fines herbes and cook, stirring frequently, for about 10 minutes or until the mushrooms have begun to exude their liquid and soften. Season with salt and pepper.

Add the flour, stirring to blend, and cook for an additional couple of minutes to allow the flour to be blended into the liquid and the raw flour taste to mellow.

Remove from the heat, stir in the cream, and season with nutmeg and, if necessary, additional salt and pepper. Pour an equal portion of the mixture into each of the prepared ramekins and sprinkle an equal portion of the cheese over each one. Place the ramekins on a rimmed baking sheet and set aside.

Heat a large cast-iron frying pan over high heat. When very hot, remove the chops from the marinade and season with salt and pepper. Working in batches, place the chops in the hot pan and sear for 3 minutes or until golden brown. Turn and sear the remaining side for about 3 minutes or until golden brown.

Continued

Transfer the pan to the preheated oven along with the gratins. Bake for about 10 minutes or until an instant-read thermometer inserted into the thickest part of the chops reads 135°F, the edges are bubbling, and the cheese is golden brown on the gratins.

Allow the chops to rest for 5 minutes so that the internal temperature will rise to 145°F. The meat should still be pink and juicy in the center.

Turn the ramekins upside down on each of 6 warm dinner plates. If the gratins do not pop out, turn right side up and run a small sharp knife around the edge and then reinvert. Lay a chop next to each one and sprinkle chives over the top. Serve immediately.

VEAL CUTLETS WITH ARUGULA SALAD

Serves 6

1½ cups Wondra flour

2 large eggs

¼ cup milk

2 cups panko bread crumbs

Salt and pepper

12 small veal cutlets, about ⅜ inch thick

¼ cup canola oil

6 large handfuls baby arugula (or other small salad green), well washed and dried

3 tablespoons extra-virgin olive oil

Juice of ½ lemon

Lemon quarters for drizzling

Simple, easy, and quick—a cook's dream. You can also use chicken or pork cutlets or, if you are feeling flush, try veal chops. Veal chops have a rib bone and rib meat surrounding the flavorful rib-eye portion of meat. To use chops, trim all of the meat and fat from the rib bone to make a "handle." Then pound the rib-eye meat to flatten lightly. The meat won't be as thin as a cutlet, so it will need a few more minutes to cook.

Preheat the oven to 200°F. Line a baking sheet with parchment paper.

Arrange 3 large shallow dishes in a straight line. Place 1 cup of the flour in the first dish. Combine the eggs and milk in the second dish and whisk to blend well. Combine the bread crumbs and remaining ½ cup flour in the final dish; season with salt and pepper to taste and stir to blend.

Working with one piece of veal at a time, dip into the plain flour, then into the egg mixture, allowing excess liquid to drip off. Then dredge both sides in the bread crumb mixture, pressing down slightly to ensure that the crumbs adhere to the meat.

Heat the canola oil in a large frying pan over medium-high heat. When very hot but not smoking, add a few of the cutlets, without crowding the pan. Fry, turning once, for about 4 minutes or until crisp and golden brown. Transfer to a double layer of paper towels to drain. Carefully transfer the cutlets to the parchment-lined sheet and place in the preheated oven to keep warm while you continue frying the remaining cutlets. If the oil gets too dark and filled with bits of the cooked coating, pour it out, wipe the pan clean with a paper towel, and start again with fresh oil.

When all of the veal is cooked, place 2 cutlets on each of 6 warm dinner plates. Place the arugula in a mixing bowl and drizzle with the olive oil and lemon juice. Season with salt and pepper and mound an equal portion on top of the cutlets on each plate. Serve with a lemon quarter for drizzling on the meat.

PORK LOIN
WITH ORANGES

Serves 6

---

4 large organic oranges

¼ cup extra-virgin olive oil

2½ pounds boneless
pork loin roast

Salt and pepper

½ cup dry white wine

2 large yellow onions,
trimmed and cut crosswise
into 8 slices each

4 bay leaves

2 tablespoons chopped
fresh chives

In the United States we are just beginning to enjoy heritage pork, but in Tuscany one of the most amazing pigs, the Cinta Senese, has been reared in the traditional way, providing the meat used in *salumi* production as well as for many wonderful meals. This dish, based on a traditional Tuscan one using the ancient breed, is a classic example of traditional home cooking at its best. However, for the flavor to reflect tradition, heritage pork is required.

Preheat the oven to 350°F.

Wash 2 of the oranges well and pat dry. Trim both ends slightly and then cut each orange crosswise into 8 slices. Set aside. Juice the remaining 2 oranges and then strain the juice through a fine mesh sieve, discarding the solids. Set the juice aside.

Heat the olive oil in a flameproof roasting pan over very low heat, without stirring, for a couple of minutes or until very warm.

Season the pork with salt and pepper and place, fat side down, in the roasting pan. Sear, turning frequently, for about 10 minutes or until nicely browned on all sides.

Raise the heat and add the wine. Cook, without stirring, for about 5 minutes or until the wine has completely evaporated.

Add the reserved orange slices and the onion slices along with the orange juice to the pan. Add the bay leaves and season with additional pepper.

Cover the roasting pan with foil and roast the pork for about 45 minutes or until the meat is very tender and an instant-read thermometer inserted into the thickest part reads 145°F. You may want to check the meat occasionally as you don't want the cooking liquid to evaporate. If it does begin to dry out, add water, no more than ¼ cup at a time.

Remove from the oven, uncover the pan, and allow the pork to rest for 10 minutes.

Using a sharp chef's knife, cut the meat crosswise into thin slices. Arrange the slices, slightly overlapping, down the center of a platter and spoon the oranges and onions around the meat. Drizzle the entire platter with the pan juices and serve sprinkled with chives.

GRILLED **PORK CHOPS** WITH RUM-MAPLE BARBECUE SAUCE

Serves 6

1½ cups dark rum

¼ cup salt

¼ cup sugar

3 cups ice cubes

6 center-cut pork chops, about
2 inches thick (see Note)

Canola oil for rubbing the chops

Salt and pepper

Rum-Maple Barbecue Sauce
(recipe follows)

Between the advertising campaign that made pork "the new white meat" and the extraordinary expansion of local/sustainable husbandry, heritage pork has become one of the current trendsetting meats. We now have Kurobuta, Mangalitsa, Duroc, Ossabaw, and Red Wattle among the heritage breeds coming to the market. I find all of them superb in flavor and texture and far superior to commercially bred hogs. At my annual Pigs & Pinot festival (see Pigs & Pinot, page 114), you will find many of these pork varieties featured in pairings with great pinot noir wines.

In Northern California we have Marin Sun Farms in Petaluma raising and selling many of the heritage breeds. In New York, the most in-demand pork comes from Flying Pigs Farm of Washington County, available at the Union Square Greenmarket.

Combine the rum with 1 quart cold water in a large (2-gallon) resealable plastic bag. Add the salt and sugar and seal. Set aside, shaking occasionally, for about 10 minutes or until the sugar and salt have dissolved. Add the ice cubes and let them melt for a few minutes.

Place the chops in the iced brine. Seal the bag and place in a large bowl (or any container large enough to hold it) to catch any leaks. Transfer to the refrigerator and brine for about 4 hours, but no more than 6 hours.

When ready to cook, preheat the grill to high and oil it.

Remove the chops from the brine and pat dry. Rub the chops with oil and season with salt and pepper.

Place the chops on the grill and close the lid. Grill for 90 seconds; then turn, re-cover, and grill the other side for another 90 seconds. If using charcoal or wood fire, move the chops to the cooler part of the grill; if using gas, lower the temperature to medium. Re-cover and grill for another 4 minutes.

Uncover, turn the chops, and, using a pastry brush, lightly brush the tops with barbecue sauce. Continue grilling, turning frequently and continually brushing with a light touch of the sauce, for about

15 minutes or until an instant-read thermometer inserted into the thickest part reads 145°F and the chops are nicely glazed.

Transfer to a serving platter and lightly tent with aluminum foil. Allow to rest for about 7 minutes to allow the meat to relax and the juices to flow.

Serve with extra sauce on the side.

Notes: If you can find them, "bacon cut" pork chops are great on the grill as they still have some of the pork belly attached.

Because of improved breeding and butchering techniques, pork is now cooked to a much lower temperature than in the past. An internal temperature of 145°F should produce meat that is tender and juicy yet can be safely eaten.

RUM-MAPLE BARBECUE SAUCE

Makes about 5 cups

1 cup dark rum

1 cup maple syrup

1 cup cider vinegar

1 cup tomato ketchup

½ cup tightly packed light brown sugar

¼ cup Dijon mustard

2 tablespoons Worcestershire sauce

¾ cup finely chopped onion

1 teaspoon minced garlic

1 teaspoon fresh thyme leaves

Cayenne pepper

Salt and pepper

Combine the rum, syrup, vinegar, ketchup, sugar, mustard, and Worcestershire sauce in a large heavy-bottomed saucepan over medium heat. Add the onion, garlic, and thyme and bring to a simmer. Lower the heat and season with cayenne, salt, and pepper. Cook, stirring occasionally, for about 30 minutes or until thick.

Remove from the heat and allow to cool. Store, covered and refrigerated, for up to 1 month.

Pigs & Pinot

Pigs & Pinot is a celebratory weekend I host at my Hotel Healdsburg. It usually occurs in March and brings together the country's most prolific pork and wine professionals, toasting and tasting their way to determine the winner of the coveted Pinot Cup. We host a series of intimate dining and educational events as a cast of master sommeliers and international celebrity chefs get together to showcase some of the world's greatest pinot noir wines with delicious pork pairings. Proceeds from the event benefit Share Our Strength as well as other local scholarships and charities.

PORCHETTA

Serves 6 to 10

1 (7-pound) boneless
pork loin, with the belly and
skin attached, butterflied
(see Note for substitution)

Grated zest of 1 large
organic orange

3 tablespoons minced garlic

2 tablespoons chopped fresh
rosemary needles

1 tablespoon Espelette pepper

Sea salt and cracked black pepper

2 tablespoons cornstarch

Porchetta is a traditional Italian dish that began as a whole pig, boned, stuffed, and roasted on a spit. In recent years it has become very popular with artisanal butchers and rustic Italian restaurants in America. You can usually find it on my or another chef's menu at my annual Pigs & Pinot gathering (see Pigs & Pinot, page 114). I use what is called a *porchetta cut*, a whole pork loin with the belly and skin attached (see Note). Porchetta makes a terrific sandwich on a ciabatta roll, particularly if you have any of the wilted cabbage (see Caramelized Onion and Cabbage Go-Withs, page 118) left over to pile on it.

Place the loin, skin side down, on a clean work surface. Using a kitchen fork, prick the meat so that it will absorb the seasoning. Flip and, using a small sharp knife, score the flap in a crosshatch pattern. Using a meat mallet, pound the entire piece of meat to even it out and tenderize. Again flip the meat so that the scored skin side is down.

Combine the orange zest, garlic, rosemary, and Espelette pepper in a small mixing bowl. Season with salt and then rub the mixture over the meat. Place on a rimmed baking sheet, cover with plastic wrap, and refrigerate for at least 8 hours or overnight.

When ready to cook, preheat the oven to 300°F.

Remove the meat from the refrigerator, uncover, and pat off any moisture with a paper towel. Lightly dust the inside of the flap with cornstarch and tightly roll the roast up, cigar-fashion, with the meaty part on the inside and the scored skin on the outside. Using butcher's twine, tie the roast tightly at 2-inch intervals. Generously season the exterior with salt and pepper.

Place on a rack in a large roasting pan and transfer to the preheated oven. Roast, frequently basting with the melting fat, for about 3 hours or until an instant-read thermometer inserted into the thickest part reads 165°F.

Let rest for about 15 minutes before cutting crosswise into 1-inch-thick slices.

Continued

Note: When purchasing the pork loin ask for a *porchetta* cut, which is now frequently available from quality butchers and some supermarkets. If you can't find the cut, purchase a pork loin and a large rectangular cut of pork belly. Then trim each piece to the same size so that the belly piece will evenly fit around the loin. Before rolling the roast, season the loin and place it on top of the belly, then wrap the belly around it.

Caramelized Onion and Cabbage Go-Withs

I usually serve porchetta with caramelized onions and a quick cabbage sauté.

To make 2 cups of caramelized onions, cut 5 large onions, lengthwise, into slivers. Combine 2 tablespoons butter and 1 tablespoon extra-virgin olive oil in a large heavy-bottomed frying pan over medium-low heat. When very hot, add the onions along with 1 teaspoon sugar and salt to taste. Using tongs, spread the onions out in an even layer and let them begin to brown for about 10 minutes before stirring or tossing. Then cook, stirring occasionally, for about 15 minutes or until golden brown. Lower the heat and continue to cook, stirring a bit more frequently, for another 15 minutes or until deep brown and well caramelized. Just before removing from the heat, stir in 1 tablespoon of balsamic or sherry vinegar to add extra sweetness.

For the cabbage sauté, I cut a medium head of cabbage (core removed) into shreds and sauté it in a bit of the fat that has cooked out of the porchetta for about 4 minutes or just until slightly wilted. Season with salt and pepper and quickly get it out of the pan to keep it from cooking further.

Wine Pairing: Pinot noirs. All of my favorite pinot noirs are from Sonoma County simply because there is something so terrific about drinking wine produced in your own backyard. They're such nutty, versatile grapes that in turn make for very easy food pairing, but they are particularly pleasing partners for all types of pork. Some of my favorite pinots are Charlie Clay, Merry Edwards, Rochioli, and Kosta Browne.

LEG OF LAMB
WITH HERBS AND ROASTED GARLIC

Serves 6

¼ cup extra-virgin olive oil

Grated zest and juice of 1 lemon

1 tablespoon chopped fresh
rosemary

2 teaspoons fresh thyme leaves

2 teaspoons celery seed

7-pound bone-in leg of lamb

About 10 cloves garlic, peeled,
cut in half if large

Salt and pepper

3 shallots, finely chopped

½ cup chicken stock or canned
nonfat, low-sodium chicken broth

¼ cup dry white wine

1 tablespoon unsalted butter,
at room temperature

1 tablespoon chopped fresh chives

I think everyone has a favorite way of roasting a leg of lamb—mine is quite simple. Make any number of slits in the flesh and fill each one with a clove of garlic. If you want to create an entire dinner in the roasting pan, add some potatoes, carrots, turnips, parsnips, or onions or whatever you like in with the lamb. Just remove them before you make the sauce.

Preheat the oven to 450°F.

Combine the oil with the lemon zest and juice, rosemary, thyme, and celery seed in a small bowl.

Using a small sharp knife, make small, random slits in the flesh of the lamb. Fill each slit with a piece of garlic. Using your hands, generously coat the outside of the lamb with the oil mixture, patting it into the meat. Season generously with salt and pepper.

Place the seasoned meat on a rack placed in a flameproof roasting pan. Roast for 40 minutes. Reduce the oven temperature to 375°F and continue to roast for another hour or until an instant-read thermometer inserted into the thickest part reads 135°F for medium-rare (or roast for about another 15 minutes to 150°F for medium).

Transfer the lamb to a serving platter, lightly tent with aluminum foil, and allow to rest for 10 minutes before carving. Note that the lamb will continue to cook while it rests, with the temperature rising about 10 degrees.

Transfer the roasting pan to the stovetop over medium heat. Add the shallots and cook, stirring up the browned bits from the bottom of the roaster, for about 3 minutes. Stir in the chicken stock and wine and bring to a boil. Boil, stirring frequently, for about 5 minutes or until the liquid has become sauce-like. Stir in the butter, taste, and, if

necessary, season with salt and pepper. Remove from the heat and stir in the chives.

Using a carving knife, cut the lamb into thin slices and serve with a bit of the sauce drizzled over the top. Pass the remaining sauce as you serve.

Wine Pairing: Château de Beaucastel Châteauneuf-du-Pape, earthy and meaty with hints of tar and dried herbs, a perfect complement to lamb.

GRILLED **DOUBLE LAMB CHOPS** WITH ROASTED GARLIC–CARROT MASH

Serves 6

6 double-cut rib lamb chops, about 4 ounces each

¾ cup extra-virgin olive oil

½ cup red wine vinegar

2 teaspoons dried Greek oregano (see Note)

Cracked black pepper

Salt

Roasted Garlic–Carrot Mash (recipe follows)

Although you can pan-sear lamb chops, I think that grilling brings out the best in them. I particularly like them after a long marination in oil and vinegar. I use Greek oregano since lamb is so associated with Greek cooking. The sweet carrot side dish seems to be the perfect complement to the aromatic lamb.

Place the lamb chops in a large shallow baking dish large enough to hold them in a single layer.

Combine the oil, vinegar, oregano, and cracked pepper in a small bowl, whisking to blend. Pour the oil mixture over the chops. Cover with plastic wrap and marinate in the refrigerator for 8 hours or overnight.

About an hour before you are ready to grill, remove the chops from the refrigerator and allow to come to room temperature.

When ready to cook, preheat and oil the grill or a stovetop grill pan.

Remove the chops from the marinade and season with salt. Transfer to the preheated grill, cover, and grill, turning once, for about 10 minutes or until an instant-read thermometer inserted into the thickest part reads 135°F for medium-rare (or about another 7 minutes to 150°F for medium). Remove from the grill and allow to rest for 5 minutes before serving with the carrot mash on the side.

Note: If you can't find dried Greek oregano (which is milder than other oreganos), combine 3 parts dried marjoram with 2 parts dried oregano for a similar flavor.

Continued

2 tablespoons unsalted butter

½ cup finely diced onion

1½ pounds carrots, peeled, trimmed, and cut crosswise into thin slices

Salt and pepper

1 cup chicken stock or canned nonfat, low-sodium chicken broth

4 cloves roasted garlic (see Note on page 28)

ROASTED GARLIC–CARROT MASH

Preheat the oven to 375°F.

Heat the butter in a heavy-bottomed saucepan with a lid over medium-low heat. Add the onion and cook, stirring occasionally, for 3 minutes. Stir in the carrots and season with salt and pepper. Cook, stirring occasionally, for about 10 minutes or just until the carrots are starting to color. Add the stock and garlic, cover, and braise in the oven for about 20 minutes or until the carrots are very tender.

Using a potato masher, vigorously mash the carrots; they don't have to be super-smooth. Taste and, if necessary, season with salt and pepper.

Serve with any grilled or roasted meat or poultry.

BAKED LEMON
CHICKEN

Serves 6

4 lemons, preferably organic

½ cup Wondra flour

½ teaspoon smoked paprika

Salt and cracked black pepper

6 bone-in, skin-on chicken breasts

2 tablespoons canola oil

1 cup chicken stock or canned nonfat, low-sodium chicken broth

1 tablespoon chopped fresh flat-leaf parsley

1 teaspoon chopped fresh mint leaves

Chicken with lemon is one of my favorite go-withs. This is a very simple recipe that works for an everyday meal as well as for entertaining. If 4 lemons seems like too many for your taste, you can temper them by replacing 1 or 2 of the lemons with an equal number of oranges, tangerines, or blood oranges. However, I find that when roasted, lemons become sweeter than you would imagine, so I urge you to at least give the original a try before adding sweeter citrus to the mix. The baked chicken stands alone but is also nice over rice, noodles, or potatoes.

Preheat the oven to 375°F.

Zest and juice 2 of the lemons and separately set aside. Cut the remaining 2 lemons into quarters and set aside.

Combine the flour with the lemon zest, paprika, salt, and cracked pepper in a shallow bowl. Dip both sides of the chicken breasts into the seasoned flour.

Heat the oil in a large nonstick, ovenproof frying pan over medium-high heat. When very hot but not smoking, add the chicken pieces, skin side down. Sear for about 4 minutes or until the skin is nicely colored. Turn the chicken and remove the pan from the heat.

Pour the excess fat from the pan. Add the chicken stock along with the reserved lemon juice to the pan, shaking to evenly distribute. Nestle the lemon quarters among the chicken and transfer the pan to the preheated oven. Bake for about 20 minutes or until the chicken is cooked through and the liquid is sauce-like. Taste and, if necessary, add salt and pepper.

Place the chicken on a serving platter. Stir the parsley and mint into the pan sauce and pour over the chicken to serve.

DEVILED CHICKEN THIGHS

Serves 6

12 skinless, bone-in chicken thighs (or drumsticks)

1½ teaspoons garlic powder

Salt and coarse ground pepper

⅔ cup mayonnaise

3 tablespoons Dijon mustard

2 tablespoons lemon juice

1½ tablespoons hot pepper sauce (such as Tabasco)

1 tablespoon prepared horseradish

1 tablespoon Worcestershire sauce

1 teaspoon cayenne pepper

2 cups dried bread crumbs (see Note)

⅓ cup chopped fresh flat-leaf parsley

1 teaspoon smoked paprika

In my early cooking days, many chefs would take the bones from a standing beef rib roast and turn them into "deviled beef bones" as a way of using meaty bones that would have otherwise been discarded. This is my take on that old-fashioned recipe. Sometimes I do a combination of thighs and legs and serve them with blue cheese dressing and celery sticks—reminiscent of another spicy chicken dish, Buffalo wings.

Preheat the oven to 375°F. Set out a large nonstick rimmed baking sheet or line a regular rimmed baking sheet with either a silicone liner or parchment paper.

Rinse the chicken and then pat very dry. Combine the garlic powder with salt and pepper in a small bowl. Using your fingertips, generously season both sides of each piece with the garlic powder mixture and place the seasoned chicken in a large bowl.

Blend the mayonnaise, mustard, lemon juice, hot pepper sauce, horseradish, Worcestershire sauce, and cayenne in a medium mixing bowl. Pour over the chicken and toss to coat well.

Combine the bread crumbs with the parsley and smoked paprika in a large shallow bowl. Working with one piece of chicken at a time, roll in the bread crumb mixture, taking care to coat completely. As coated, place in a single layer on the prepared baking sheet.

Bake the chicken for about 35 minutes or until the juices run clear and the exterior is golden brown and crisp. Serve.

Note: For this recipe, don't use fresh bread crumbs. You need the dry, commercially packaged bread crumbs that are finer than homemade. Don't, however, use flavored bread crumbs as this recipe has more than enough seasoning.

CHICKEN PAILLARDS
WITH KALE AND BLOOD ORANGE SALAD

Serves 6

2 blood oranges

1 bunch kale, tough stems removed

½ cup bias-cut scallions

6 boneless, skinless chicken breast halves

¾ cup Wondra flour

Salt and pepper

¼ cup olive oil, plus 3 tablespoons more if necessary

2 shallots, minced

½ cup chicken stock or canned nonfat, low-sodium chicken broth

1 tablespoon Dijon mustard

When studying at the Culinary Institute of America, I learned that *paillard* was French for a thin piece of veal that was usually fried. The term is now loosely used to describe what we also call a cutlet and may refer to any type of meat, but it is usually still fried. And doesn't chicken paillards sound a whole lot fancier than fried chicken cutlets? You'll find this recipe fancy enough for a dinner party yet simple enough for an everyday meal.

Zest the oranges and set the zest aside. Using a sharp knife, carefully trim a small slice off of the top and the bottom of each orange to keep it stable as you cut. Then remove the remaining peel and pith from the oranges. Using a small knife and holding the orange over a bowl, carefully insert the knife against a membrane separating the individual segments, cutting all the way down to loosen the segment. Then press the knife under the segment and cut up against the membrane on the other side of the orange segment to loosen it completely. Let the segment drop into the bowl. Continue separating segments in this fashion until all of the segments are released and you are left with connected membranes. Squeeze the membranes to get the last drop of juice. Discard the membranes. Repeat with the remaining orange.

Drain the orange segments through a fine mesh strainer, separately reserving the juice and the segments.

Stack a few kale leaves at a time and roll them up, cigar-fashion. Using a sharp knife, cut the roll crosswise into very thin slices. Pull the slices apart and you should have ribbons of kale. Repeat to slice all the kale and then place in a large salad bowl. Add the reserved orange segments and the scallions and toss to coat.

Working with one breast at a time, place the chicken between 2 sheets of plastic wrap. Using a cast-iron skillet or meat mallet, pound the meat until it is about ½ inch thick.

Place the flour in a shallow bowl and season with salt and pepper.

Continued

Press both sides of each paillard into the seasoned flour, shaking off excess.

Heat the ¼ cup oil in a large frying pan over medium-high heat. Add the floured chicken and fry, turning once, for about 10 minutes or until golden brown, crisp, and cooked through. Remove to a warm platter and tent lightly with aluminum foil to keep warm.

If most of the oil has been absorbed by the chicken, add 3 tablespoons oil to the hot pan. Keeping the pan on medium-high heat, add the shallots and stir, scraping the bottom of the pan to release all of the browned bits. Add the chicken stock along with the reserved orange zest and juice and bring to a boil. Lower the heat, whisk in the mustard, season with salt and pepper, and cook for about 3 minutes or until slightly thickened.

Remove from the heat and pour the dressing over the kale, tossing to coat the kale so that it wilts slightly.

Mound an equal portion of the salad on each of 6 dinner plates. Place a warm paillard on top and serve.

Wine Pairing: Etienne Sauzet White Burgundy, rich and complex with high acidity that won't overpower the paillards but will stand up to the strongly flavored kale.

TURKEY MARSALA

Serves 6

3 tablespoons olive oil

2 cups sliced mushrooms, either button or cremini

Salt and pepper

½ cup chicken stock or canned nonfat, low-sodium chicken broth

1 cup Wondra flour

6 to 8 turkey cutlets

¾ cup Marsala wine

3 tablespoons unsalted butter

1 tablespoon chopped fresh flat-leaf parsley

Rather than the traditional veal or the popular chicken, I use turkey cutlets to make my version of Marsala. Growing up, the only turkey I knew was the wild turkey that my dad and brothers hunted or the big supermarket bird that my mom cooked at Thanksgiving. Like my dad, I still hunt and fish and try my best to bag one of the now-bountiful-but-still-elusive wild birds in season. But I will admit that it doesn't happen very often. With whole turkey (and many cuts and pieces) available all year long, and heritage birds finding their way to the table more and more, you don't have to go into the wilds to have a wonderful turkey dinner.

Heat 1 tablespoon of the oil in a large frying pan over medium heat. Add the mushrooms and season with salt and pepper to taste. Cook, stirring frequently, for about 5 minutes or until the mushrooms have exuded their liquid and are beginning to brown.

Lift the pan and carefully drain off excess oil. Return the pan to medium heat and add the chicken stock. Bring to a simmer, lower the heat, and cook at a bare simmer for 3 minutes. Remove from the heat and keep warm.

Combine the flour with salt and pepper in a large shallow bowl. Working with one piece at a time, press both sides of the turkey cutlets into the seasoned flour, shaking off excess.

Heat the remaining 2 tablespoons oil in a large frying pan over medium-high heat. When very hot but not smoking, add the floured cutlets. Fry, turning once, for about 10 minutes or until the cutlets are golden brown on both sides and just cooked through. Transfer to a warm platter, tent lightly with aluminum foil, and keep warm.

Drain the oil from the pan and return the pan to medium-high heat. When very hot, add the Marsala and carefully ignite by tipping the pan to the side so that the burner's flame can touch the wine. It should ignite quickly. Lift the pan from the fire and let the flame die out. If you do not have a gas stove, you can use a long match such as those used for fireplaces to ignite the wine.

Return the pan to medium heat and add the reserved mushrooms, stirring to blend. Then stir in the butter and season with salt and pepper. Bring to a simmer, stirring to scrape up any brown bits from the bottom of the pan.

Pour the mushroom sauce over the turkey, sprinkle with parsley, and serve.

HONEY-SMOKED
WHOLE TURKEY

Serves a crowd

3½ cups raw honey
(see Note)

2 cups dry white wine

1 cup orange juice

1 large onion, chopped

1 tablespoon fresh thyme leaves

1 tablespoon fresh
rosemary needles

1 tablespoon whole allspice

1½ cups salt

½ cup black peppercorns

1 (20-pound) heirloom turkey,
rinsed and patted dry

½ cup canola oil

If you don't have a backyard smoker, I urge you to get one; it will make entertaining so easy throughout most of the year. You don't have to stand by it throughout the cooking process as you do with a grill, so you can do chores or party while dinner cooks. With poultry, I like to use whatever wood chips reflect the flavors I have used in the brine, but if there is no defining flavor, I will always opt for fruitwoods, such as apple or pear.

Combine 3 cups of the honey with the wine and orange juice in a large brining bag (large enough to hold the turkey). Add the onion, thyme, rosemary, and allspice, seal the bag, and squish to blend and allow the honey to incorporate into the liquid.

Open the bag and add about 1 gallon of ice water along with the salt and peppercorns. Again, seal the bag and let the salt dissolve.

When the salt has dissolved, add the turkey. Seal and refrigerate for at least 8 hours but no more than 24 hours.

Prepare your smoker following the manufacturer's directions for smoking a turkey.

Combine the remaining ½ cup honey with the oil in a small bowl, stirring until completely blended.

Remove the turkey from the brine, brush off any herbs or spices that cling to the skin, and pat it dry.

Using your hands, rub the entire turkey with the honey-oil mixture. Place in the smoker and smoke according to the manufacturer's directions for a 20-pound bird.

When it is fully cooked, remove and let rest 30 to 45 minutes. Carve and serve as you would a roasted bird.

Note: As unbelievable as it may seem, in New York City beekeepers are now harvesting honey from hives kept on rooftops throughout the five boroughs and selling their excellent honey at various farmers markets in the city. Brooklyn Grange has a particularly good reach. In Sonoma County, we have a number of wonderful local honeys, ranging from a mix of wildflowers to lavender-scented. Among them are Bear Foot Honey Farm, Bloomfield Bees, and Lavender Bee Farm, but you can also find raw honey at most specialty food stores and farmers markets.

LONG ISLAND
DUCK BREAST WITH
CITRUS COUSCOUS

Serves 6

6 boneless Long Island duck
breast halves, 6 to 8 ounces
each (see Note)

1 tablespoon canola oil

Grated zest of 1 lemon

½ teaspoon ground juniper berries

¼ teaspoon pepper, plus
more as needed

3 tablespoons Chartreuse (see
The Charm of Chartreuse, page 136)

Salt

Grated zest and juice of
1 small orange

¼ cup (½ stick) unsalted butter,
at room temperature

¾ cup heavy cream

1 tablespoon chopped fresh chives

Citrus Couscous
(recipe follows)

Once in a while I come inside and cook up a restaurant-style dish for my family and friends. This is one of them: a bit rich between the fatty duck and the cream, but it certainly is delicious. It combines a classic look at duck with what was, in my early days, an almost unknown grain in American cooking—couscous.

Remove the skin from each duck breast half and reserve.

Place the skinless breasts in a resealable plastic bag. Add the oil along with the lemon zest, juniper berries, and pepper. Add 1 tablespoon of the Chartreuse, seal the bag, and vigorously massage to evenly coat the breasts with the seasoning. Set aside for 30 minutes.

Place the duck skin in a large frying pan over medium-high heat. Fry, stirring occasionally, for about 15 minutes or until all of the fat has rendered out and the skin is very crisp. Transfer the skin to a double layer of paper towels to drain. Once drained, break into small pieces and set aside.

Pour off all but about 1 tablespoon of the duck fat and return the pan to medium-high heat. Remove the breasts from the marinade, season with salt, and place in the hot pan. Sear, turning once, for about 6 minutes or until an instant-read thermometer inserted into the thickest part reads 125°F for very rare or 135°F for medium-rare. (Most chefs now serve duck breast very rare, taking it out of the pan at about 122°F, with the rest time bringing it up to a very rare temperature.) Place the breasts on a warm plate and tent lightly with aluminum foil to keep warm for 5 minutes while you finish the sauce.

Lower the heat under the pan and add the remaining 2 tablespoons Chartreuse, stirring for about a minute or so to deglaze the pan. Add the orange juice and butter, stirring to blend well. Add the cream, raise the heat slightly, and bring to a simmer. Season with salt and pepper and simmer for about 5 minutes or until reduced and slightly thickened. Remove from the heat and stir in the orange zest and chives.

Place a mound of couscous to the side of each of 6 warm dinner plates.

Continued

Working with one piece at a time and using a sharp knife, cut the breasts crosswise on the bias, keeping the breast intact as you cut. When ready to plate, put your knife under the sliced breast and, using your other hand to hold the top together, transfer to the center of the couscous on each plate. Once plated, pull the knife back toward you so that the breast stays in place but the slices open slightly.

Drizzle the pan sauce over each breast and the couscous and around the edge of the plate. Garnish with a few pieces of the crisp duck breast skin sprinkled over all.

Note: Long Island duck (also called American Peking duck) has been bred over many, many generations on farms located throughout Suffolk County, Long Island, New York. At one point, there were hundreds of farms, but environmental issues and rapidly rising real-estate costs have limited the farms to just a few. One of the longest lasting and finest is Crescent Duck Farms in Aquebogue.

CITRUS COUSCOUS

2 tablespoons unsalted butter

1 shallot, finely chopped

2½ cups chicken stock or canned nonfat, low-sodium chicken broth

¼ cup orange juice

2 tablespoons lemon juice

Salt and pepper

2 cups couscous

Grated zest of 1 lemon

For this recipe you can use any couscous (except Israeli), whether marked *instant* or not, since the grains have been precooked and this recipe will have sufficient liquid and cooking time.

Melt the butter in a medium saucepan over medium heat. Add the shallot and cook, stirring frequently, for about 2 minutes or just until softened. Add the stock along with the orange and lemon juices. Season with salt and pepper and bring to a boil. Immediately add the couscous and return to a boil. Lower the heat to its lowest possible setting, cover, and cook for about 5 minutes or until all of the liquid has been absorbed. Let rest, covered, for 5 minutes.

Uncover, add the lemon zest, and use a fork to fluff the grains and incorporate the zest. Serve as directed in the recipe or as a side dish or base for vegetable salads.

The Charm of Chartreuse

Chartreuse is a very flowery, aromatic, almost-sweet herbal liqueur produced by Carthusian monks in the French Alps. It is made using an ancient recipe steeping a secret mix of herbs in neutral alcohol. The alcohol is distilled and aged for 5 years in oak vats. It comes in green and yellow, with the yellow being the least alcoholic and the sweetest.

CHAPTER 6

FISH

Growing up in a rural community, I often ate fish that was caught by my dad in local streams and lakes. As an adult I became a fisherman myself, enjoying both the sport of it and the flavor and quality of a freshly caught fish on the plate. I have gone bonefishing in the Caribbean, caught trout in New York's Delaware River, and line fished for salmon around Orcas Island of Washington State. In fact, everywhere I go I try to get in some fishing. Deep-sea, surf casting, bonefishing, fly-fishing—you name it and I've tried my hand at it. And, of course, once I've caught something, I like nothing better than to cook it—sometimes simply and sometimes extravagantly. I offer some wonderful fish dishes below, but don't hesitate to do nothing more than simply grill a freshly caught whole fish or a beautiful fillet or steak, seasoned only with a little salt and pepper and drizzled with lemon and extra-virgin olive oil.

SAN FRANCISCO
CRAB BOIL

Serves 6

1 bottle light beer, plus more if needed

1 lemon, cut in half crosswise

1 tablespoon peppercorns

6 bay leaves

6 Dungeness crabs

Sourdough baguette, warmed and cut crosswise into thick slices

Lemon wedges for serving

Cocktail Sauce (recipe follows)

This is a classic. Not original, but worth repeating as there is nothing quite like a San Francisco crab boil at home. You can add whatever condiments you like, but you have to have newspapers on the floor, sourdough bread, and cocktail sauce. The fun is watching each person develop their own technique as they work hard at snagging bits of meat from the crabs with their crackers and picks.

Fill the largest stockpot you have with cold water. Place over high heat and add the beer, lemon halves, peppercorns, and bay leaves. Bring to a boil.

Once boiling, use tongs to lift the crabs and add as many as you can to the boiling water, leaving plenty of room for the water to boil around them. Return the water to a boil and then lower the heat to medium-high and simmer for about 15 minutes or until the crabs are bright red-orange and cooked through.

Lift the cooked crabs from the water and rinse under cool running water. Continue to cook the crabs until all are done, adding water and, if desired, more beer as necessary.

Cover the table and floor with newspaper.

Working with one crab at a time, place it belly side up on a cutting board and lift up and break off the triangular piece of shell at the tail of the crab (the apron) and discard it. Then place your thumb in the spot from which you have removed the apron and give a pull to lift and discard the top shell from the body. Using a sharp chef's knife, cut each crab in half straight down the center.

Wrap the warm sourdough in a clean kitchen towel and place in a bread basket or big wooden bowl.

Place the crab halves in the middle of the newspaper along with crab crackers, picks, and mallets. Place the lemon wedges among the crab and give each diner a bowl of Cocktail Sauce. Let everyone fend for themselves, either eating the crab as it is or piling their pickings on a slice of warm sourdough bread, drizzling with lemon juice, and dressing with the sauce.

Continued

2 cups chili sauce
(such as Heinz)

¼ cup well-drained horseradish
(or to taste)

2 tablespoons lemon juice

2 teaspoons hot pepper sauce
(such as Tabasco)

1 teaspoon Worcestershire sauce

COCKTAIL SAUCE

Makes 2½ cups

Combine all of the ingredients in a small mixing bowl. Cover and refrigerate until ready to use. Will keep, covered and refrigerated, for 1 week.

Wine Pairing: I can't think of anything better to drink with this rustic dish than a very lush and luxe white burgundy such as Puligny-Montrachet from Etienne Sauzet. You will certainly impress your drinking buddies.

CIOPPINO

Serves 6 to 8

½ cup olive oil

6 large cloves garlic, sliced

2 onions, chopped

1 leek (with some green part), well washed and chopped

1 carrot, peeled and minced

1 red bell pepper, cored, seeded, and diced

2 (28-ounce) cans San Marzano tomatoes, cut into pieces, with their juice

1 cup canned tomato sauce

2 tablespoons chopped fresh flat-leaf parsley, plus more for garnish if desired

2 tablespoons chopped fresh basil leaves

1 teaspoon dried thyme

1 teaspoon dried oregano

1 (8-ounce) bottle clam juice

½ cup dry white wine

Salt and black pepper

Red pepper flakes

1 pound firm-fleshed fish, such as bass, snapper, or halibut, cut into bite-sized pieces

1 to 2 Dungeness crabs, cracked into pieces

1 dozen clams

1 pound peeled and deveined shrimp

½ pound scallops

Cioppino is a shellfish stew that I discovered in San Francisco. It probably had its origins with the southern Italian immigrants who were often fishermen on the wharf. It is very similar to all Mediterranean fish stews in that as long as you have a flavorful tomato base, you can add almost any fish or shellfish you like. Cioppino is a terrific dish to feed a crowd—perfect for a New Year's celebration or a Sunday football gathering. Of course, if you want to honor the Italian tradition of a Christmas Eve meal featuring seven fishes, this mix could fit the bill if you make sure to add enough varieties.

Heat the olive oil in a soup pot over medium heat. Add the garlic, onions, leek, carrot, and bell pepper and cook, stirring frequently, for about 5 minutes or until the vegetables begin to soften. Add the tomatoes, tomato sauce, parsley, basil, thyme, and oregano, stirring to blend. Add the clam juice and wine, season with salt, black pepper, and red pepper flakes, and bring to a simmer. Cook at a low simmer for 40 minutes or until the flavors have blended nicely. (You can make the base up to this point, cool, and store, covered and refrigerated, for up to 3 days. Reheat before serving.)

About 20 minutes before you're ready to serve, return the base to a boil. Add the fish and cook for 5 minutes. Then add the crab and clams and return to a simmer. Cook for 5 minutes or just until the clams begin to open slightly. Add the shrimp and scallops and cook for another 5 minutes.

Remove from the heat and ladle into individual large shallow soup bowls or one large soup tureen. Garnish with parsley, if desired, and serve with warm bread for sopping up the delicious broth.

CHERMOULA-GRILLED
SALMON

Serves 6

6 (7-ounce) skin-on salmon fillets

Canola oil for brushing

Chermoula (recipe follows)

Lemon wedges for serving, optional

Chermoula, a garlicky North African sauce, is often paired with fish and shellfish in Tunisia, Algeria, and Morocco. I discovered it when traveling and embraced it as my own. I'm not a real chile lover, so I add only one to my mix, but feel free to add more if you like to feel your tongue on fire. Chermoula is one of those cook's specialties that can be made with any number of combinations of herbs and spices, but it almost always has garlic, oil, and cilantro. It is a very tasty sauce to have on hand; it keeps well and adds a kick to grilled meats as well as fish. It is particularly suited to offsetting the rich fattiness of salmon.

Preheat and oil the grill, or preheat the oven to 450°F.

Using a pastry brush, lightly coat the skin side of the salmon with canola oil; if roasting the salmon in the oven, lightly coat a baking sheet with canola oil and do not oil the fish. Generously coat the flesh side of the salmon with ½ cup of the chermoula.

If grilling, transfer the salmon, skin side down, to the hot grill, cover, and grill for about 12 minutes or until the skin is crisp and the salmon is barely cooked—the center should remain almost raw. If necessary, halfway through the cooking, carefully transfer the fish to a cooler side of the grill. If roasting in the oven, transfer the chermoula-coated fish to the prepared baking sheet, place in the preheated oven, and roast for about 10 minutes or until cooked as above.

Serve immediately with a bowl of the remaining chermoula and lemon wedges on the side.

Note: For an entirely different look and texture, mix about ¼ cup fresh bread crumbs with the ½ cup chermoula. It will become a thick paste that can be molded to the top of each piece of salmon, making a crisp, spicy topping. If you do this, it is best to roast the salmon.

Continued

10 cloves garlic, peeled

1 red hot chile, stemmed and seeded

1 cup fresh flat-leaf parsley leaves

1 cup fresh cilantro leaves

2 tablespoons lemon juice

1 tablespoon grated orange zest

¾ cup extra-virgin olive oil

2 tablespoons red wine vinegar

2 tablespoons tomato paste

2 teaspoons ground toasted cumin

2 teaspoons sweet paprika

Salt

Cayenne pepper

CHERMOULA

Makes 2 cups

Combine the garlic, chile, parsley, cilantro, lemon juice, and orange zest with ½ cup cool water in the bowl of a food processor fitted with the metal blade. Process to a smooth puree.

Scrape the puree into a medium saucepan. Add the oil, vinegar, tomato paste, cumin, and paprika, stirring vigorously to blend. Place over medium heat and cook, stirring constantly, for about 5 minutes or until the mixture comes to a simmer. Season with salt and cayenne and cover loosely. Simmer, stirring occasionally, for 5 more minutes or until it reaches a sauce-like consistency. If too thick, add water, a tablespoonful at a time.

Transfer to a nonreactive container. Set aside to cool. When cool, use as directed in a specific recipe or store, covered and refrigerated, for up to 2 weeks.

STRIPED BASS
STUFFED WITH CRAB
AND MUSHROOMS

Serves 6

1 large fennel bulb, trimmed
of tough stalks and any
bruising and cut lengthwise
into very thin slices

1 large sweet onion, cut crosswise
into very thin slices

2 tablespoons extra-virgin olive oil

Salt and pepper

¼ cup dry white wine

2 tablespoons canola oil

2 shallots, minced

3 tablespoons finely minced celery

3 cups chopped wild mushrooms

2 teaspoons chopped fresh tarragon

2 teaspoons chopped fresh chives

4 teaspoons lemon juice

2 (3-pound) striped bass, cleaned,
with heads on

¾ pound Dungeness or
lump crabmeat

2 tablespoons chopped fresh
flat-leaf parsley

1 teaspoon hot paprika

Chopped fresh tarragon or flat-leaf
parsley for garnish, optional

Lemon slices for serving, optional

For years, I have been an avid bass fisherman. When I caught bass I knew it was as fresh as it could possibly be, so I would generally cook it simply—usually in the oven, occasionally on the grill. But, of course, being a chef, "simple" got a bit boring, so over the years I have devised other preparations. This is one of my family's favorites, and it is easy to do with so much Dungeness crab available in Northern California. In New York, I might use chopped lobster or shrimp instead.

Preheat the oven to 450°F.

Combine the fennel and onion with the olive oil in a large bowl, tossing to coat well. Season with salt and pepper and transfer to a roasting pan large enough to hold the fish. Add the wine and bake for about 15 minutes or just until slightly tender. Set aside.

Heat 2 teaspoons of the canola oil in a large frying pan over medium heat. Add the shallots and celery and cook, stirring frequently, for about 3 minutes or just until softened. Add the mushrooms, season with salt and pepper, and cook, stirring, for another 5 minutes or just until the mushrooms have exuded some of their liquid but have not colored. Remove from the heat and stir in the tarragon and chives. Season with salt and pepper and transfer to a mixing bowl. Set aside to cool.

Mix the remaining canola oil with 2 teaspoons of the lemon juice and salt and pepper in a small bowl. Using a pastry brush, lightly coat both the interior and the exterior of each fish with the seasoned oil.

When the mushroom mixture has cooled, add the crab to it, along with the remaining 2 teaspoons lemon juice, the parsley, and the paprika, tossing to mix well.

Place an equal portion of the crabmeat stuffing into the cavity of each fish, pressing down slightly to close.

Lay the stuffed fish on top of the fennel/onion mixture in the pan, leaving space in between. Roast for about 22 minutes or until

Continued

an instant-read thermometer inserted into the thickest part of the fish reads 135°F.

Remove the pan from the oven and allow the fish to rest for 5 minutes. Then, using two spatulas, carefully lift each fish from the roasting pan onto a serving platter. Spoon the fennel-onion mixture around the fish and, if desired, garnish with chopped tarragon or parsley and fresh lemon slices. Serve immediately.

Wine Pairing: When serving fish, sauvignon blanc is the wine I most frequently turn to. It also makes a lovely aperitif. Daryl Groom, my close friend and Sonoma neighbor, delivers his sauvignon blanc vintage to us from his family's winery in Australia. Groom and Mauritson are a couple of my favorite sauvignon blanc wines.

ONION-PEPPER CRUSTED
TUNA STEAKS

Serves 6

1 cup dehydrated or dried onion

¼ cup crushed black peppercorns

Sea salt

1 large egg white

6 (7-ounce) 1½-inch-thick tuna steaks

1 tablespoon grapeseed oil

1 large red bell pepper, cored, seeded, membrane removed, and cut lengthwise into thin strips

1 large yellow onion, cut lengthwise into thin strips

⅓ cup sliced kalamata olives

2 tablespoons capers, well drained

1 tablespoon fresh oregano leaves

¼ cup dry white wine

1 tablespoon lemon juice

Salt and pepper, optional

About 2 tablespoons extra-virgin olive oil

1 bunch arugula, tough stems removed

1 head radicchio, cored and cut lengthwise into shreds

I have been making some version of this dish for many years. It was originally on an early menu I created for Periyali, a Greek restaurant in Manhattan that I owned with Steve Tzolis and Nicola Kotsoni. The recipe works very well with swordfish or halibut, and the sauce can also be used with sautéed chicken breasts.

Combine the dehydrated onion with the ¼ cup crushed black peppercorns and sea salt in a small shallow bowl.

Place the egg white in a small bowl and, using a whisk, beat until frothy. Using a pastry brush, lightly coat both sides of the tuna steaks with the egg white. Quickly dip both sides of each steak into the onion mixture.

Heat the oil in a large nonstick frying pan over high heat. Add the tuna steaks and sear, turning once, for about 4 minutes for medium-rare. Transfer to a warm platter.

Immediately add the bell pepper and onion to the hot pan. Cook, stirring frequently, for about 3 minutes or just until softened. Add the olives, capers, and oregano and cook for another minute. Stir in the wine and lemon juice and cook for another 3 minutes or until the pan juices have reduced somewhat. Taste and, if necessary, season with salt and pepper. Add a drizzle of olive oil and remove from the heat.

Combine the arugula and radicchio in a mixing bowl, tossing to blend. Place an equal mound of the salad on each of 6 dinner plates. Place a warm tuna steak on top and spoon the pepper sauce over the top. Serve immediately.

GARLIC **SHRIMP**

Serves 6

2 pounds jumbo (U15) shrimp
(see Note on page 45), peeled
and deveined, tails on
....
Grated zest and juice of 1 lemon
....
¼ cup extra-virgin olive oil
....
¼ cup (½ stick) unsalted
butter, melted
....
¼ cup dry white wine
....
3 tablespoons minced garlic
....
Salt and pepper
....
2 tablespoons chopped fresh
flat-leaf parsley
....
Garlic Bread, optional
(see page 176)
....

I like to use huge meaty shrimp for this recipe, but if you can't find
them, use any size you like. It is the garlicky sauce that is the star here.
I've found that children (or maybe it's just boys), more than almost
anything, love to have a handle to hold on to and a sauce to dip into
when they eat. This recipe takes it to the max with tail-on shrimp and
is even better with some crusty bread to dunk.

Preheat the broiler.

Arrange the shrimp in a single layer in a shallow baking dish.
Set aside.

Combine the lemon zest and juice, olive oil, butter, wine, and garlic
in a small saucepan over medium heat. Bring to a simmer, lower the
heat, and cook at a bare simmer for 3 minutes or until the garlic has
softened. Season with salt and pepper and pour over the shrimp.

Place the baking dish under the preheated broiler and broil the
shrimp for about 4 minutes or until bright pink and a little charred
around the edges.

Remove from the broiler, fold in the parsley, and spoon into a serving
bowl. If desired, serve with Garlic Bread or crust peasant bread to dunk
and absorb the juices.

RUM-SCENTED
LOBSTER WITH ORZO

Serves 6

3 cups orzo

4 tablespoons (½ stick)
unsalted butter

Salt and white pepper

2 large shallots, minced

Pinch saffron threads

1½ tablespoons Wondra flour

1½ cups sliced fresh morels
or other wild mushrooms

1½ cups heavy cream,
at room temperature

4 large egg yolks,
at room temperature

6 tablespoons light rum

4 cups cooked lobster meat

2 teaspoons fresh thyme leaves

1 teaspoon fresh chervil leaves

2 tablespoons chopped
fresh chives

If you are going to eat lobster any way other than steamed or off the grill, it should be extra rich and luscious. This recipe is just that. I use orzo as the base for the rich lobster sauce, but you could use rice or another pasta or any mild grain. This recipe will also work very well with large shrimp or scallops.

Cook the orzo according to package directions. Drain well and return to the pan. Add 1 tablespoon of the butter and season with salt and white pepper. Cover and keep warm.

Melt the remaining 3 tablespoons butter in a medium saucepan over medium heat. Add the shallots, saffron, and a pinch of salt. Cover and cook for 3 minutes or until the shallots are soft and translucent.

Uncover and, using a wooden spoon, stir in the flour. Cook, stirring constantly, for about 2 minutes or until a light roux has formed but the mixture has not browned. Add the morels and sauté for another 3 minutes. Whisk in the cream and season with salt and pepper to taste. Cook, stirring constantly, for about 5 minutes or until thickened.

Place the egg yolks in a small bowl and whisk until light and frothy. Whisking constantly, add a bit of the hot cream sauce to the yolks to temper them. Then whisk that yolk mixture back into the hot sauce. Add the rum and return the mixture to low heat. Fold in the lobster meat and cook for just a couple of minutes to heat through. Taste and, if necessary, add additional salt and pepper.

Place an equal portion of the orzo in the center of each of 6 large shallow soup bowls. Fold the thyme and chervil into the lobster sauce and then spoon an equal portion over the orzo in each bowl. Sprinkle with chives and serve.

MUSSELS IN CHORIZO-TOMATO BROTH

Serves 6

5 pounds mussels in the shell

1 (28-ounce) can chopped San Marzano tomatoes with their juice

6 ounces Spanish chorizo, cut into small cubes

1 cup dry white wine

3 cloves garlic, thinly sliced

1 teaspoon fresh thyme leaves

Large pinch saffron

Pepper

Crusty bread or Garlic Bread (page 176)

I once saw an elegant woman in Paris eat her mussels by graciously pushing the meat from the shell with another shell. I taught my boys to do this and it got them eating mussels, not quite so graciously, but certainly with a vengeance. This recipe makes a light broth that is delicious on its own, thanks to the slightly spicy chorizo and the scent of the sea from the mussels. You do need some crusty bread, a green salad, and some chilled white wine, perhaps something from the Loire, or a Dry Creek sauvignon blanc.

Clean the mussels by scrubbing them in a sink full of cold water. Pull off any beards that remain. Discard any mussels that remain open and place the remainder in a large soup pot.

Combine the tomatoes with the chorizo in a large bowl. Add the wine, garlic, and thyme, stirring to blend well. Add the saffron and pepper and then pour the tomato mixture over the mussels.

Place the pot over high heat, cover, and bring to a boil, shaking the pan occasionally to move the mussels around. Cook for about 5 minutes or until all of the mussels have opened. Discard any mussels that have not opened as they might be tainted.

Ladle an equal portion of the mussels, along with the broth, into each of 6 large shallow soup bowls.

Serve immediately with crusty bread to sop up the broth.

CHAPTER 7

FAMILY FAVORITES AND BACKYARD DINNERS

No matter your family or its ethnicity, you likely have a number of dishes that have become classic favorites, ones that are served over and over again. These dishes are not only satisfying, but they also make people happy. (Interestingly, this is also true in restaurants, where a signature or popular dish can never be taken off the menu as customers will complain and demand that it come back.) Favorite dishes are usually very tasty and, when you eat them often enough, you develop a taste for the particular flavors they hold. Sometimes you have a family favorite because of culinary heritage, and sometimes it is because of flavors you have experienced and liked. And sometimes we leave home and discover that the dish we loved growing up really isn't very good, yet still we continue to make it because it brings up deep food memories that evoke love, comfort, and family.

The dishes in this chapter are my family's favorites—the ones I grew up with and the ones my family asks for over and over again.

Backyard dinners have been part of my life since I was a kid in upstate New York. Winters there are long, snowy, and sometimes abysmally gray, and the summers are short—so we welcome spending time outdoors in the sun. My mom loved nothing better than to gather her extended clan together for a backyard barbecue where her chicken and speidies (a traditional upstate kabob) were always on the menu, along with potato salad and coleslaw and lots of local brew. Nowadays the local brew is great Belgian-style beer from Brewery Ommegang outside Cooperstown, New York; in my day, it was Genesee or Genny Light brewed in Rochester. But no matter the brew, it was my mom's enthusiasm for outdoor cooking that stuck with me.

In California, we now have outdoor dinners as often as we can using my wood-fired oven or the grill. Outdoor dinners can be as simple as grilling up some burgers with their fixings for everyone to put together as they please, or as fancy as our Wood-Roasted Chipotle Oysters (page 42). A couple of our favorites come from my mom: She was not considered a great cook, but she had a recipe or two that we all loved and still make, like the oatmeal cookies my kids love. They are pretty much straight off the Quaker oatmeal box, but with a little twist on my part. Other dishes are our own, and although they might have a bit of restaurant influence, they really are dishes that any home cook can turn into a personal family favorite.

BREAKFAST **CREPES**

Makes about 30 crepes

6 large eggs

1½ cups all-purpose flour

1 tablespoon sugar

1 teaspoon salt (or to taste)

2 to 2½ cups nonfat milk

3 tablespoons unsalted
butter, melted

1 teaspoon pure vanilla extract

2 pounds shredded cheddar cheese

1½ pounds thinly sliced
smoked ham, cut into strips

Savory ham-and-cheese crepes, and of course sweet chocolate crepes, have become a go-to breakfast on Saturday mornings when our house is filled with high school football players after a Friday night under-the-lights game. I've become quite famous for my breakfast burritos with this crew, but when time is a consideration, these crepes come together within minutes. By using two pans, I can get them out almost as quickly as the boys can eat them. With a sunny-side-up egg on top, the dish is known as the Slammer.

Once they've had their fill of ham-and-cheese crepes, I swap to a filling of 1 ounce (about 2½ tablespoons) of milk chocolate chips. I finish these sweet crepes off with a dusting of confectioners' sugar before I pass them along to reached-out hands. When the chaos is over, Lisa and I enjoy a chocolate crepe with a good cup of coffee.

If you want to work as quickly, as I do, you will need 2 nonstick 10-inch crepe pans.

Place the eggs in a medium mixing bowl. Stir in the flour, sugar, and salt and, mixing constantly, begin adding the milk in a slow, steady stream. When you've added about half of the milk, the batter should loosen, at which point you can slowly begin adding some of the remaining milk along with the melted butter and vanilla. The batter should be of a coating consistency, similar to half-and-half, so you may not need all of the milk.

Preheat two 10-inch nonstick crepe pans over medium heat. Lightly coat each one with nonstick cooking spray. Using a small ladle, pour just enough crepe batter (about ¼ cup) into one pan to coat the entire bottom of the pan. Take the pan off the heat and lift and swirl it until the batter has spread to evenly coat the bottom.

Immediately return the pan to the heat and sprinkle the crepe with about 2 tablespoons of cheese followed by about 1½ tablespoons of ham. (At this point, begin making another crepe in the other hot pan.)

Continued

Cook for about 45 seconds to a minute or until the bottom is golden brown. Using a silicone spatula, gently fold the crepe in half and then fold the half into quarters.

Flip the folded crepe out onto a plate and serve as you go. Continue making crepes until there are no more hungry mouths to feed.

....

Notes: When making your first crepe, the batter might stick to the pan and tear when you attempt to turn it. This indicates that the pan has not been properly seasoned, or that there is a bit of residue from past crepe-making in the pan. Often, the first crepe (and even the second one) will stick because the heat is not correct, but all subsequent ones should pop right out. If the crepe looks as though it is pulling inward quickly, this indicates that the pan is too hot. If it doesn't set up almost immediately, the pan is too cold. All of this sounds daunting, I know, but it really does become easy once you get started.

If you want to make the crepes in advance, place a parchment paper–lined baking sheet in a 200°F oven. As each crepe finishes cooking, transfer it to the baking sheet to keep warm. Do not stack the crepes; keep them in a single layer.

If you have extra batter, continue making the crepes without any filling, flipping them over after 45 seconds to just set on the other side, 5 to 10 additional seconds. Slide them off onto a plate and begin stacking them. Once cool, wrap tightly and keep in the fridge. They're great rolled with any type of filling. The kids like to sprinkle them with sugar and fresh lemon juice, and then pop them into the microwave for 10 seconds.

FONTINA
FRITTATA TART

Serves 6

1 pound lean, smoky bacon
(see Artisanal Bacon, below),
cut into small pieces

2 leeks, well washed and
trimmed (white with some
green part), chopped

10 large eggs, at
room temperature

½ cup crème fraîche

1½ cups (about 6 ounces) grated
fontina cheese

Salt and pepper

½ recipe Short Pastry for Tarts
and Pies (recipe follows),
fit into a 10-inch tart pan

This is the Palmer family Christmas morning tradition. We like the tart at room temperature with salsa on the side, but it is also delicious warm and cheesy just out of the oven. Wrapping paper flies as the boys open their gifts, while Lisa and I enjoy our strong coffee and sit back to enjoy the show and wait for the tart to come out of the oven.

Preheat the oven to 350°F.

Place the bacon in a large frying pan over medium-low heat and fry, stirring occasionally, for about 12 minutes or until all of the fat has rendered out and the bacon bits are crisp. Using a slotted spoon, transfer the bacon to a double layer of paper towels to drain.

Pour off all but about 1 tablespoon of the bacon fat. Return the pan to medium heat and add the leeks. Cook, stirring occasionally, for about 5 minutes or just until the leeks have sweat their liquid. Using a slotted spoon to allow excess fat to drip off, transfer the leeks to a medium mixing bowl. Let cool slightly.

Add the eggs to the leeks and whisk vigorously to combine. Then whisk in the crème fraîche followed by the cheese. When blended, season with salt and pepper.

Pour the egg mixture into the tart shell. Scatter the bacon bits over the top. Bake for about 1 hour or until the center is set and the top and the pastry are golden brown.

Set on a wire rack to cool for about 10 minutes before cutting into wedges and serving.

Artisanal Bacon

We have an extraordinary bacon right in our California backyard. It comes from Black Pig Meat Co. in Healdsburg. It is sweet yet salty, very meaty, and carries a primo amount of smoke. There are now artisanal bacons being produced all across the country, but if you don't find one locally, I'm sure there are any number of suppliers (such as Nodine's Smokehouse, D'Artagnan, Newsom's Country Ham, and Nueske's) who will have it on your doorstep overnight via the Internet. If all else fails, both Trader Joe's and Whole Foods offer premium applewood-smoked bacons.

Continued

2½ cups all-purpose flour,
sifted

½ teaspoon salt

1¼ cups (2½ sticks) plus
1 tablespoon unsalted butter,
cubed and chilled

½ cup ice water

Wondra flour for rolling
the dough

SHORT PASTRY FOR TARTS AND PIES

Makes enough for 2 tart shells or 1 double-crust pie

This pastry recipe is for a perfect all-purpose dough. You can add a teaspoon of sugar to the mix when making sweet pies or tarts; you can also use lard for meat-based mixes and a mixture of butter and vegetable shortening for a less-rich dough.

Combine the flour and salt in the bowl of a food processor fitted with the metal blade. Process to aerate and blend.

Add the butter and, using quick on-and-off turns, process just until crumbly. With the motor running, slowly add the water and process just until the dough begins to pull into a ball. Scrape the dough from the processor bowl, divide in half, and form each piece into a flat disk. Wrap in plastic wrap and refrigerate for about 30 minutes to chill before rolling. The dough may also be frozen; thaw before using.

Place a light dusting of Wondra flour on a clean, flat work surface and on the rolling pin. Place the dough in the middle of the floured surface and, using a very light hand, begin rolling out from the center, lightly coating it and the rolling pin with Wondra if the dough wants to stick. Gently lift the rolling pin as you near the edge to prevent breakage. Roll until you have a circle about 2 inches larger than the size of your pan.

Lift the dough by gently folding it in half over the rolling pin. Then place it, still folded, into the tart (or pie) pan. Carefully unfold it so that it covers the bottom of the pan. Try not to pull or stretch the dough, or it will shrink away from the sides of the pan during baking. If the dough tears, gently pinch it back together or patch the hole with leftover dough. Smooth the dough down into the pan and up the sides with quick pressing movements. For a tart, trim off excess dough around the edge. For 2-crust pies, leave the excess dough so you can crimp both the bottom and the top together once the bottom shell is filled.

Use as directed in a specific recipe.

PALMER KITCHEN
CHICKEN LIVER PÂTÉ

Makes four 8-ounce jars

1 tablespoon grapeseed oil

1 onion, chopped

2 cloves garlic, minced

¼ pound very lean bacon, cut into small pieces

18 ounces chicken livers

¼ cup port wine

Salt

Pinch ground cinnamon

7 ounces chicken fat (schmaltz; see Note)

Over the years I should have learned not to expose the boys to so much restaurant dining, as they always managed to find something on the menu that they wanted to make at home. This is a classic example—a French bistro, a basket of garlic toasts, and a small ramekin of smooth, smooth chicken liver pâté to quiet the hunger of our young kids while we enjoyed an aperitif and ordered dinner. Of all the things you wouldn't expect boys to eat, a liver pâté has to be high up on the list. But the Palmer boys devoured it, asked for more, and then insisted that I teach them how to make it at home.

Since the pâté is processed in a boiling water bath, use small round European-style canning jars with an airtight-seal lid, a replaceable rubber gasket, and a metal clamp to hold the lid in place. They also serve as very attractive containers that can go straight to the table.

Heat the oil in a large frying pan over medium heat. Add the onion and garlic and cook, stirring frequently, for about 5 minutes or until beginning to color. Stir in the bacon and cook for about 3 minutes. Add the chicken livers and cook, stirring frequently, for about 12 minutes or until nicely browned. Scrape the mixture into the bowl of a food processor fitted with the metal blade.

Raise the heat to high under the frying pan. Add the port wine and bring to a boil, stirring constantly to scrape up any browned bits from the bottom of the pan. Boil for about 4 minutes or until the wine has become syrup-like. Using a rubber spatula, scrape the pan juices into the processor bowl.

Season the chicken liver mixture with salt and cinnamon. Add half of the chicken fat and process until quite smooth. (Here's where you can get fancy if you want: For perfectly smooth pâté, you can push the pureed mixture through a very fine mesh sieve. It will take some work, but it will be almost as smooth as butter.)

Transfer the mixture to four 8-ounce canning jars.

Melt the remaining chicken fat in a small saucepan over low heat.

Continued

When melted, pour an equal amount over the top of each filled jar to completely cover. Seal the jars.

Place the filled jars on a rack in a large saucepan or canning pot with water to cover by at least 3 inches. Place over high heat and bring to a boil. Cover and boil for 1 hour, making sure that the jars remain completely covered with water.

Remove the jars from the water bath and place on a wire rack to cool before storing in a cool, dark place or in the refrigerator.

Serve straight from the jar with crisp toasts—either plain or garlic-flavored.

Note: Rendered chicken fat is also known by its Yiddish name, schmaltz. It is typically used in the cooking practices of Eastern and Middle European Jews, but in recent years, schmaltz, along with lard, has moved into contemporary American cooking. It is very rich and caloric, but when used to fry it lends an almost sweet flavor to the food being fried. You can make it yourself by rendering chicken skin, or it may be purchased in the refrigerated kosher section of most supermarkets or, of course, online.

ERIC'S BAKED
LITTLENECK CLAMS

Makes 2 dozen

2 dozen littleneck clams

Coarse salt

Rock salt (see Note)

Compound Butter
(recipe follows)

1 cup fresh bread crumbs

24 (1-inch) square pieces
(about 6 slices) lean bacon

2 lemons, cut into small
wedges, for serving

This is another recipe that evolved from a restaurant experience. Eric, one of my twin boys, ordered Clams Casino and was so disappointed with the bready, tasteless mix that came to the table that he decided to make baked clams his specialty at home. Although we help shuck, this is Eric's own recipe and we are all his sous chefs. He has done such a good job that his version has become one of the family's favorite snacks at cocktail time on the deck.

Discard any clams that remain open when tapped.

Fill a large bowl with cold water and add about ¼ cup coarse table salt. Set aside.

Using a stiff kitchen scrub brush, scrub each clam under cold running water to clean thoroughly. As cleaned, transfer the clams to the salted water and let them cleanse for about 15 minutes. Repeat the cleansing 2 more times using fresh cold water and salt. This is to ensure that all of the sand is eliminated from the clams.

Preheat the oven to 400°F.

Line 2 shallow baking dishes (we use a 6-quart Staub cocotte or casserole) with a ½-inch layer of rock salt. If you don't have shallow baking dishes, use baking sheets lined with a ½-inch layer of rock salt. Set aside.

Place a thick glove on your nondominant hand and a clam-shucking knife in your dominant hand. Working with one clam at a time, place it in the palm of your gloved hand and hold on to it. With the clam level with the shucking knife, insert the tip of the knife in between the shell, next to the hinge at the back. Using the knife as leverage, twist into the shell to pry it apart. You will hear a sharp noise as the shell opens. Do not force it open or the shell will crack. Holding the clam firmly and evenly, gently twist the knife to open the shell entirely. Still keeping the bottom shell level (you don't want to lose the juice), cut the muscle at the hinge to detach the clam from the shell. Discard the top shell.

Continued

Nestle the clam into the salt on the prepared baking sheet and continue opening clams until all are open.

Place a slice of compound butter on top of each clam. Sprinkle an equal portion of bread crumbs over the top of each clam and then place a piece of bacon on top.

Bake for about 12 minutes or until the bacon is cooked and the bread crumbs are golden brown.

Serve immediately with lemon wedges to squeeze over the top of the hot clams.

Note: If you don't have rock salt or can't find it, you can use an equal amount of coarse or kosher salt.

COMPOUND BUTTER

Makes 1 cup

1 cup (2 sticks) unsalted butter, at room temperature

1 shallot, minced

1 tablespoon chopped fresh chives (or flat-leaf parsley, basil, or tarragon)

1 teaspoon fresh lemon juice

Salt and pepper

Combine the butter, shallot, chives, lemon juice, salt, and pepper in the bowl of a food processor fitted with the metal blade and process to thoroughly blend.

Using a rubber spatula, scrape the butter into the center of a piece of plastic wrap (or waxed paper). Fold the wrap over the butter and, using your hands, form the butter into a neat log about 1½ inches in diameter. Tightly close the ends of the plastic wrap and transfer the log to the refrigerator. Chill for at least 1 hour or until firm, or freeze for up to 3 months.

When ready to use, unwrap the log and cut the butter crosswise into ¼-inch-thick slices. Use as directed in a specific recipe.

REED'S **BRUSCHETTA**

Makes about 30

About 3 tablespoons extra-virgin olive oil

1 large baguette (see Artisanal Bread, below), cut crosswise into ¾-inch-thick slices

Garlic salt

Pepper

1 small yellow onion, finely chopped

1 tablespoon minced garlic

2 cups canned diced San Marzano tomatoes, well drained

1 teaspoon chopped fresh oregano

Small block of Parmesan cheese, for shaving

Reed, one of our twins, hates raw tomatoes but loves bruschetta, so he devised his signature dish using canned San Marzano tomatoes. The result is a sweet, herby toast that we all love. I don't know if he will decide to make food his career, but he is certainly inventive when left on his own in the kitchen.

Preheat the oven to 350°F. Line a rimmed baking sheet with parchment paper.

Using a pastry brush and about 2 tablespoons of the olive oil, lightly coat one side of each baguette slice. Season with garlic salt and pepper. Lay the slices, seasoned side up, on the prepared baking sheet. Bake for about 10 minutes or until golden brown. Keep warm.

Heat the remaining 1 tablespoon olive oil in a large sauté pan over medium heat. Add the onion and garlic and cook, stirring frequently, for about 5 minutes or until just beginning to color. Immediately add the tomatoes and oregano and cook for another 4 minutes or just until hot and well flavored.

Using a slotted spoon, generously cover the top of each slice of warm seasoned toast with the tomato mixture. Immediately shave some Parmesan over the top and serve warm. (Once topped, do not allow the bruschetta to sit too long or the toast will get soggy.)

Artisanal Bread

Americans producing great artisanal breads across the country have, I believe, now surpassed bakers in Europe in skill and innovation. In the 1970s we wouldn't have believed this. Starting with a quiet revolution of a few individual bakers trying their hand at producing European-style breads, artisanal bread baking created a flour storm as more and more bakeries came to life all across the country. By the 2000s, bakeries were thriving in both urban and rural communities, and even supermarkets were doing the finishing of par-baked baguettes and other breads, filling stores with the aroma of sourdough and rye. Now, in New York City there are any number of bakeries bringing dense, crusty European-style breads to the market, among them Amy's Bread and Sullivan Street Bakery. In Sonoma, we have Wildflower Bread Company, among others, turning out magnificent loaves from wood-fired ovens. And, even in my restaurants, particularly Aureole in Manhattan, our chefs are creating breads that were once unimaginable in a restaurant setting.

LENTIL–BUTTERNUT SQUASH **SOUP**

Serves 6 to 8

3 tablespoons unsalted butter

3 leeks (white and some light green part), well washed and finely chopped

2½ quarts vegetable broth or chicken stock or canned nonfat, low-sodium vegetable or chicken broth

2 cups red lentils, rinsed

3 cups randomly diced butternut squash

2 cloves garlic, peeled

2 teaspoons minced fresh thyme

1 teaspoon minced fresh tarragon

Salt and pepper

Garlic Bread (recipe follows)

Here's an easy soup to put together quickly that can be made for vegetarians or just about anyone who's in need of a warm and hearty soup. Rustic and filling, it's perfect to nourish the body on a chilly winter day, which we definitely have in New York, but also in California! My family expects a loaf of crusty bread warmed in the oven with garlic and olive oil to accompany the soup, but any warm peasant-style bread will do.

Heat the butter in a large soup pot over medium heat. Add the leeks and cook, stirring frequently, for about 5 minutes or just until they have sweat their liquid. Add the stock and lentils, raise the heat, and bring to a boil. Lower the heat and cook at a gentle simmer for about 15 minutes or until the lentils are turning to mush. Stir vigorously to smooth out the lentils.

Add the squash, garlic, thyme, and tarragon and return to a simmer. Season with salt and pepper and continue to simmer, stirring occasionally, for about 20 minutes or just until the squash is tender but still holds its shape.

Remove and discard the garlic. Serve hot with garlic bread.

GARLIC BREAD

1 large baguette

3 cloves garlic, chopped

¼ cup extra-virgin olive oil

¼ cup (½ stick) butter, at room temperature

¼ cup fresh flat-leaf parsley leaves

Coarse ground pepper

¾ cup grated Parmesan cheese

Preheat the oven to 400°F. Line a baking sheet with a silicone liner or parchment paper.

Using a bread knife, cut the bread in half lengthwise. Place the bread, cut side up, on the prepared baking sheet.

Combine the garlic with the oil, butter, parsley, and pepper in the bowl of a food processor fitted with the metal blade. Process until well combined but with bits of parsley still evident. You don't want a totally green mixture.

Using a sandwich spreader, spread an equal portion of the garlic mix on each piece of bread. Sprinkle an equal portion of the cheese on top of each piece. Bake for about 12 minutes or until the tops are golden brown.

Cut the bread crosswise into thick slices. Place in a towel-lined bread basket and serve hot.

CHICKEN **PICCATA**

Serves 4

---

4 split (2 whole) boneless skinless chicken breasts, about 8 ounces each

About 2 tablespoons olive oil, plus more if necessary

Salt and pepper

About ¼ cup Wondra flour

3 tablespoons unsalted butter, at room temperature, plus more if necessary

1 cup dry white wine

2 tablespoons fresh lemon juice (about 1 large lemon)

2 tablespoon capers packed in salt, rinsed and coarsely chopped

2 tablespoons chopped fresh flat-leaf parsley

This is a starred dinner for my boys. Sometimes I make it in the classic Italian way using veal, but we all love the chicken version just as much. When everyone is hungry and time is of the essence, a piccata is a great dinner as it takes only a few minutes to bring to the table. If you think ahead, you can flatten the chicken early in the day, place it between sheets of parchment paper, and refrigerate until ready to cook.

I generally double this recipe because my guys are healthy eaters. This is easy to do: Simply increase all of the ingredients equally. It can be served with polenta, pasta, or rice, or on a bed of sautéed greens.

Preheat the oven to 200°F.

Working with one piece at a time, place a chicken breast half on a clean, flat work surface. Using a sharp chef's knife, cut the breast in half horizontally through the center. Continue until you have 8 pieces of chicken fairly equal in size.

Cut a piece of parchment paper large enough to make a nice "rug" for the chicken. Lightly coat with some of the olive oil. Again, working with one at a time, place a piece of chicken in the center of the oiled paper. Lightly coat another sheet of parchment with oil and place it over the chicken. You shouldn't use more than 1 tablespoon olive oil for the paper as you are using it simply to keep the chicken from sticking to the paper. Using a meat cleaver or a small heavy frying pan and working from the center out, lightly pound the meat until it is an even flat piece about ¼ inch thick. Continue flattening the chicken until all pieces have been flattened. You may have to use clean sheets of parchment paper.

When all of the chicken has been flattened, season with salt and pepper and then lightly dredge both sides in the Wondra flour, shaking off any excess.

Combine 1 tablespoon each of olive oil and butter in a large heavy frying pan over high heat. When very hot but not smoking, add the seasoned chicken. Do not crowd the pan; add just as many pieces as the pan can hold without crowding. Cook for about 2 minutes or just until the bottoms have browned lightly. Turn and brown the remaining side for an additional 2 minutes or just until golden. Transfer to a baking sheet and place in the preheated oven to keep warm. Continue frying until all of the chicken has been cooked. You may need to add more butter and oil to the pan.

Pour off all but about 1 tablespoon of the fat from the pan. Add the wine and cook, stirring and scraping up the browned bits from the bottom of the pan, for about 5 minutes or until the wine has reduced by about half.

Add the lemon juice, stirring to blend. Then add the remaining 2 tablespoons butter and continue to cook until the sauce is slightly thick and smooth. Stir in the capers along with half of the parsley. Season with salt and pepper and remove from the heat.

Place the chicken on a serving platter and spoon the sauce over the top. Sprinkle with the remaining parsley and serve immediately.

MOM'S BARBECUED
CHICKEN

Serves 6

2 (3½-pound) chickens, cut into serving pieces, rinsed and patted dry

2 large eggs, at room temperature

1 cup olive oil

2 tablespoons salt

1 tablespoon Bell's Seasoning

1 teaspoon pepper

2 cups cider vinegar

Whenever and wherever the Palmer family gathers in the summer, my mom's chicken has to be on the menu. Mom's zest for living was not matched by her talent in the kitchen, but her famous chicken dish made her the reigning queen at barbecues. Although everyone asked for the recipe, she would not share it. Somehow, before Mom passed away, my sister Brenda managed to get it out of her, so Brenda is now the barbecue queen. If you manage to have any, the leftovers make a great chicken salad.

Place the chicken in a shallow glass baking dish large enough to hold it in 2 layers or less.

Combine the eggs with the oil in a medium mixing bowl, whisking until very well blended. Whisk in the salt, poultry seasoning, and pepper. When combined, whisk in the vinegar. Pour over the chicken. Cover with plastic wrap and refrigerate for at least 8 hours, but no more than 24 hours, turning the chicken from time to time to ensure that each piece is well marinated.

When ready to cook, preheat and oil the grill. You want a very low heat.

Remove the chicken from the marinade, allowing the excess to drip off. Grill, frequently turning and brushing with the marinade, for about 20 minutes or until the skin is nicely browned and the juices run clear when pierced with the point of a small, sharp knife. If the skin begins to blacken before you think the chicken is fully cooked, lower the heat if using a gas grill, or move the chicken pieces to the cooler, outer edges of a charcoal grill. (When Mom decided the chicken was cooking too fast, she would quickly transfer it to a baking pan and finish it in a 375°F oven.)

Serve hot straight off the grill or at room temperature.

CRISPY LEMON
CHICKEN CUTLETS

Serves 6

1 cup all-purpose flour

3 large eggs

2 cups panko bread crumbs

2 lemons, zest grated,
lemons quartered

Cayenne pepper

Salt and pepper

12 thin chicken cutlets

About ¼ cup olive oil

This is one of the boys' favorite recipes—thankfully, because it is so easy to make and uses ingredients that I always have on hand. I can have dinner on the table in less than 15 minutes and, if I make a big batch, there is some left over for sandwiches the next day. The acid from the lemon offers the perfect note to accent the rich, crunchy crust.

Place the flour in a large shallow bowl. Place the eggs in another large shallow bowl, add 2 tablespoons cold water, and whisk to combine. Set the bowl next to the flour. Then combine the crumbs, zest, cayenne, salt, and pepper in a final shallow bowl, stir to blend completely, and place next to the eggs.

Working with one piece at a time, place the chicken cutlets in the flour, evenly coating each side. Then dip the flour-coated chicken into the eggs, taking care that all sides are covered. Finally, press the chicken into the seasoned bread crumbs, again taking care that all sides are evenly coated in crumbs.

Heat the oil in a large frying pan over medium heat.

Place the coated chicken cutlets in the hot oil and fry, turning once, for about 10 minutes or until crisp and golden brown. Do not crowd the pan; cook the cutlets in batches if necessary. Using tongs, transfer the chicken to a double layer of paper towels to drain.

Place the cutlets on a serving platter, drizzle with the juice from the lemon quarters, and serve hot.

Note: Japanese-style panko bread crumbs are especially good for frying as they don't absorb as much grease as Western-style bread crumbs. They yield a lighter, crispier, and crunchier crust that doesn't overpower white meats and fish.

BAKED RICOTTA MEATBALLS
IN TOMATO SAUCE

Serves 6 to 8

2 cups ricotta (see Fresh Ricotta
on page 56 to make your own)

1 pound ground beef

1 pound finely ground veal
shoulder meat

2 large eggs, at room temperature

1 cup grated Parmesan cheese

¼ cup minced onion

1 tablespoon diced red bell pepper

2 teaspoons minced garlic

2 teaspoons chopped fresh
flat-leaf parsley

2 teaspoons red pepper flakes
(or to taste)

Dash Tabasco sauce

Salt and pepper

½ cup plus 2 tablespoons fresh
peasant bread crumbs

1 to 1½ quarts Tomato Sauce
(recipe follows)

Cooked spaghetti, noodles,
or rice for serving

These are about the best meatballs I've ever tasted: meaty, cheesy, and slightly spicy. The recipe makes quite a few meatballs; I often make them just to have on hand to make classic Italian meatball heroes for the family on the weekend. But if not making heroes, we usually pile them on spaghetti, but you can certainly use rice, grains, or noodles as a base.

Place the ricotta in a fine mesh sieve over a large bowl. Set aside to drain for 1 hour.

Preheat the oven to 425°F. Lightly oil a large rimmed baking sheet with olive oil.

Combine the drained ricotta with the beef and veal in a large mixing bowl. Add the eggs, Parmesan, onion, bell pepper, garlic, parsley, and red pepper flakes. Season with Tabasco, salt, and pepper. Using your hands, squish the mixture together to thoroughly blend. Add the bread crumbs and continue to squish until the bread crumbs are completely incorporated.

Place a medium bowl of cool water next to the meatball mix. Dip your hands into the water and begin forming the mixture into 1½-inch balls. As formed, place the meatballs on the oiled baking sheet.

Bake the meatballs, turning occasionally, for about 15 minutes or until just barely cooked through.

Place the tomato sauce in a large saucepan over medium heat. As soon as the meatballs come out of the oven, using a slotted spoon (to allow any excess oil to drip off), transfer the almost-cooked meatballs to the tomato sauce. Simmer in the sauce for about 15 minutes or just until the meatballs are fully cooked and the sauce has some of their flavor.

Serve over spaghetti, rice, or noodles.

Continued

¼ cup olive oil

6 cloves garlic, minced

1 large white onion, finely diced

8 large fresh basil leaves, chopped

1 teaspoon dried oregano

2 tablespoons sugar

2 tablespoons red wine vinegar

4 (28-ounce) cans chopped San Marzano tomatoes

Salt and pepper

TOMATO SAUCE

Makes about 5 quarts

Heat the olive oil in a large nonreactive saucepan over medium-low heat. Add the garlic and onion and cook, stirring frequently, for about 4 minutes or just until slightly softened. Do not brown. Stir in the basil and oregano followed by the sugar and vinegar. When blended, add the tomatoes and bring to a simmer. Season with salt and pepper and continue to cook at a low simmer, stirring occasionally to keep the bottom from burning, for 35 minutes or until well flavored.

Remove from the heat and use immediately or allow to cool and store, tightly covered and refrigerated, for up to 5 days, or freeze for up to 3 months.

BALSAMIC-SOY GRILLED **TRI-TIP STEAK**

Serves 6

⅔ cup olive oil

⅓ cup balsamic vinegar

1 tablespoon soy sauce

3 cloves garlic, minced

1 large shallot, cut crosswise into thin slices

1 tablespoon chopped fresh thyme

4 pounds tri-tip steak (see Note)

I'm not sure I even knew what a tri-tip steak (see Note) was when I left culinary school. Perhaps this is because it is a steak that goes by many names, depending upon the region of the world in which it is being served. It is not seen as frequently in New York, where it is known as a Newport or triangle steak, as it is in California. In fact, I never cooked it until I began to spend time on the West Coast. But in our house of meat-eaters, a tri-tip barbecue quickly became a favorite. By the way, the balsamic-soy marinade will work with almost any piece of beef or pork.

I often choose a Silver Oak cabernet to go with the steak. It is an easy-drinking young wine that doesn't require ten years of aging to make it an enjoyable quaff with grilled beef.

Combine the olive oil, vinegar, and soy sauce in a resealable plastic bag large enough to hold the meat. Add the garlic, shallot, and thyme, seal, and shake the bag to blend.

Add the steak, reseal, and refrigerate for at least 8 hours or up to 3 days, turning occasionally to ensure that all of the meat receives equal marination.

Preheat and oil the grill. (Alternatively, heat about 1 tablespoon canola oil in a stovetop grill pan over medium-high heat.)

When the grill (or pan) is very hot, remove the steak from the marinade, allowing the excess to drip off, and carefully place on the grill (or in the hot pan). It is best to do this by laying the steak on the grill from the front to the back. This will keep the hot oil from splattering back onto your hand. Sear for 3 minutes on one side, then turn and grill, turning occasionally, for an additional 25 minutes for medium-rare. (Stovetop grilling will take about the same amount of time.)

Transfer the steak to a cutting board and let rest for 5 minutes. Using a sharp knife, cut the steak, crosswise against the grain, into thin slices. Serve immediately.

Continued

Note: Tri-tip steak (aka Newport steak, triangular steak) comes from the bottom sirloin and gets its name from the fact that it is a triangular muscle with three tips. It usually weighs about 2½ pounds. Tri-tip is very flavorful, low in fat, and generally less expensive than other steaks. Because of its low fat content, tri-tip is only cooked to medium-rare as it tends to dry out if cooked longer. In Southern California, where it is highly seasoned or marinated and cooked over a wood fire, the steak is called a Santa Maria barbecue. It is also extremely popular in Argentina, where it is known as *colita de cuadril* and is a part of a traditional *asado* (barbecue event). In Europe, it is often boiled or roasted rather than grilled.

EIGHT-HOUR SLOW-BRAISED
PORK SHOULDER

Serves a crowd

12- to 16-pound pork shoulder
(see Note)

About 6 tablespoons canola oil

3 tablespoons coarse salt

2 tablespoons ground
chipotle chile powder

2 tablespoons paprika

2 tablespoons black pepper

1 tablespoon cayenne pepper

1 tablespoon onion powder

1 tablespoon garlic powder

1 tablespoon dried Mexican oregano

3 cups beer or ale, plus
more if needed

Pork shoulder meat is the perfect sweet, fatty meat for making pulled pork—the end result of this recipe. You can cook it in the oven (as I do here), on a grill, in a slow cooker, or in a smoker. No matter what you do, when you cook it long enough it will turn into tender, tasty goodness. Cook it too long and it will melt in your mouth, too little and you can cut it into slices. But when it is perfect, just pull it apart into long shreds, pile it on a bun, and, if you have it, add some coleslaw (see page 15), and chow down—which is what we do.

Pulled pork, another regional American dish that has spread all across the country, is found everywhere from barbecue joints, to fast-food and family-meal chains, to urban farm-to-table restaurants. The recipe originated in the South and the Southwest, with each region having its own claim to the authentic one. Some do the whole hog, some just the shoulder, some mixed parts of the pig. The sauce might be tomato-based barbecue-style, vinegar-based, or yellow mustard–based. Mine is just a mix of the seasonings and reduced beer that the meat was cooked in. On a drinking note, I always cook with the same beer I'm going to drink, and you should also. This assures that the flavors of the meat and the cold beer are harmonious.

Preheat the oven to 300°F.

Lightly coat the meat with about 2 tablespoons of the canola oil.

Combine the salt, chile powder, paprika, black pepper, cayenne, onion powder, garlic powder, and oregano in a small bowl. Stir to blend well.

Using your fingers, rub about half of the spice mix over the meat. Then drizzle 2 tablespoons of the remaining canola oil over the rub and, using your hands, knead the spice rub into all of the top surface and sides. Turn the meat over and repeat the process over the bottom of the meat with the remaining 2 tablespoons oil and spice mix.

Transfer the meat to a large heavy-bottomed Dutch oven. Add the beer, cover, and transfer to the preheated oven. Cook for 8 hours, checking from time to time to make sure there is still a bit of moisture in the pan. If not, add no more than ½ cup liquid (either water or additional beer) and continue cooking until the meat almost falls apart when you pierce it with a fork.

Let the pork rest for about 15 minutes. Then, using a kitchen fork, pull the meat apart into shreds, discarding any pockets of fat that appear as you shred. Serve as is with coleslaw (see page 15) and potato salad, or on soft rolls as a sandwich.

Note: A bit of information about pork shoulder: A true pork shoulder comprises the front leg and shoulder of a hog and should weigh anywhere from 12 to 16 pounds. The shoulder has a good amount of collagen and fat, which make it a perfect candidate for long, slow cooking or smoking, as the collagen melts into the meat and tenderizes it while the fat keeps it moist. For commercial purposes, it is usually divided into two cuts, the picnic and the Boston butt. The butt is not what the name would imply, but rather the upper section of the front shoulder. I strongly recommend that you use the whole shoulder; however, if you can't find it, you can use either the picnic or the butt, either of which should weigh anywhere from 6 to 8 pounds. Although the picnic is often sold boneless, I do recommend purchasing one with the bone remaining as it offers sweeter flavor in the cooked meat.

MUSTARD-CRUSTED
RACK OF LAMB

Serves 6

3 lamb racks, about 1¼ pounds
each, Frenched (see Note)

Salt and pepper

1½ cups fresh bread crumbs

½ cup chopped fresh
flat-leaf parsley

3 tablespoons fresh thyme leaves

1 tablespoon minced garlic

About 3 tablespoons olive oil

¼ cup Dijon mustard

Lamb is a Palmer house favorite, and when the boys were younger they particularly loved picking up the chops by the exposed bone—a little pretend caveman thing going on there. They wouldn't think of doing that now that they are men. This is a classic and elegant French dish that so easily translates to the home kitchen. Quick to make, it works for a weeknight supper or for entertaining. Lamb pairs well with Charlie Clay Russian River Valley Pinot Noir, our favorite house wine.

Preheat the oven to 450°F.

Cover the bare bones on the lamb racks with little pieces of aluminum foil to keep them from burning. Generously season the racks with salt and pepper. Set aside.

Combine the bread crumbs with the parsley, thyme, and garlic in a mixing bowl. Add just enough olive oil to moisten.

Heat a heavy-duty frying pan over high heat. When very hot, add the seasoned lamb racks, meat side down. Using a wooden spoon, tongs, or a spatula, press the meat into the hot pan so that it sears quickly and evenly. Then turn the racks so that all sides get a quick sear. This should take no more than 5 minutes.

When the racks have all been seared, use a pastry brush to generously coat the meat side with the mustard. Try to give a smooth coating. Then carefully pat an even layer of the bread crumb mixture over the mustard, pressing down to adhere to the meat.

Transfer the coated racks to a rimmed baking sheet, meat side up. Roast for about 20 minutes or until medium-rare (120°F on an instant-read thermometer). Let rest for 5 minutes.

Place on a serving platter and present at the table. Working quickly (the lamb will continue to cook and you want to keep it nice and pink), cut the racks between the bones into individual chops. Serve immediately.

Note: For a "Frenched" rack of lamb, the chine bone is removed, excess fat is cut from the meat, and the meat, fat, and sinew are scraped from the ends of the rib bones, leaving them exposed. This is done for aesthetic reasons only. It is easy to do, but most racks are now sold this way.

DIJON-GLAZED **SALMON**

Serves 6

¼ cup Dijon mustard

¼ cup honey mustard

¼ cup (½ stick) unsalted butter

2 tablespoons chopped fresh dill

1 teaspoon mustard seeds

1 teaspoon grated lemon zest

6 (7-ounce) skinless salmon fillets

Salt and pepper

In the restaurant business we used to call salmon "chicken of the sea" because it was inexpensive and easy to showcase. However, that has changed, and not only has salmon become a bit pricey, but we have quite a variety to chose from—farm-raised, wild, organic, Scottish, Alaskan, and so forth. I only buy wild, preferably Alaskan, salmon, with Copper River one of the most outstanding for both its fattiness and its flavor as well as the skill with which it is handled during netting. You can check the Monterey Bay Aquarium Seafood Watch site (seafoodwatch.org) for more information on purchasing salmon.

Slowly roasting the fish allows the salmon to just barely cook through yet remain extremely moist and flavorful. Slow cooking also gives the glaze time to adhere to the fish and really shine. The honey adds just the perfect sweetness to offset the peppery mustard and highlight the buttery sweetness of the salmon. This is one recipe that will convince any wary fish-eater to dive right in. Pun intended!

Preheat the oven to 275°F. Generously butter a shallow baking dish large enough to hold the fish without crowding.

Combine the mustards with the butter, dill, mustard seeds, and lemon zest in a small mixing bowl and, using a rubber spatula, mash to blend thoroughly.

Using a sandwich spreader (or a table knife), spread an equal portion of the mustard mixture over the top of each piece of salmon. Season with salt and pepper and transfer to the prepared roasting pan.

Roast the salmon for about 20 minutes or just until the fish is barely cooked through and the top is glazed. (If the top is not as glazed and shiny as you would like, set the oven to broil and place the fish under the hot broiler for no more than a minute.) Remove from the oven and serve.

SAUTÉED
SWISS CHARD
WITH FETA

Serves 6

3 tablespoons extra-
virgin olive oil

1 large sweet onion,
cut lengthwise into slivers

Salt

1 pound Swiss chard, tough
stems removed, chopped

Pepper

8 ounces feta cheese, diced

This dish was first introduced to us by Ferai, our extraordinary Turkish nanny. It was her attempt to get the boys to eat greens, and it quickly became a family favorite. I liked it so much that over the years we've done versions of it in all of the restaurants. It is a simple mix that works as a side dish with almost any protein.

Heat the oil in a large sauté pan over medium heat. Add the onion and season lightly with salt (noting that the cheese will add saltiness). Cook, stirring occasionally, for about 12 minutes or until the onion is golden and beginning to caramelize. Stir in the chard, season with pepper and cook, tossing and turning with tongs, for about 5 minutes or just until the chard is soft and wilted.

Remove from the heat and, using the tongs, toss in the cheese. Taste and, if necessary, season with salt and pepper. Serve immediately.

DOUBLE-STUFFED **POTATOES**

Serves 6

6 large (about 1 pound each) Idaho potatoes

About 2 tablespoons canola oil

½ pound smoky bacon, diced

3 cups (about 12 ounces) shredded sharp cheddar cheese

1½ cups sour cream

6 tablespoons unsalted butter, at room temperature

3 tablespoons chopped scallions

Salt and pepper

I know, I know—you're thinking, What's a chef doing making the proverbial steak house side of over-the-top stuffed potatoes? Well, I do own steak houses, and my boys like nothing better than steak and potatoes. So years ago I thought, Why not bring a little steak house magic home? These quickly became a family favorite, particularly when the bacon comes from one of our local purveyors (see Artisanal Bacon, page 166).

Preheat the oven to 400°F.

Using your hands, generously coat the potatoes with the canola oil. Randomly prick the skins with a kitchen fork. Place directly on the rack of the preheated oven and bake for about 1 hour or until the point of a small sharp knife easily pierces into the center. Place on a wire rack until cool enough to handle.

Place the diced bacon in a large frying pan over medium heat. Fry, stirring occasionally, for about 5 minutes or until brown and crisp. Using a slotted spoon, transfer to a double layer of paper towels to drain.

Working with one potato at a time and using a serrated knife, horizontally cut about ½ inch off each potato. Using a tablespoon, scoop out the pulp from each potato, leaving about ¼ inch of potato remaining on the interior. You should now have a potato canoe. Place the scooped pulp into a medium mixing bowl and place the potato skins on a nonstick baking sheet.

Using a potato masher, smash the potato until very smooth. Stir in 1½ cups of the cheese along with the sour cream, butter, scallions, and reserved bacon bits. Season with salt and pepper and stir until all of the ingredients have blended evenly.

Spoon the potato mixture back into the potato shells. Evenly sprinkle the remaining cheese over the top. Bake for about 20 minutes or until the cheese has melted and the potatoes are very hot. Serve immediately.

DAD'S **OATMEAL COOKIES**

Makes about 4 dozen small cookies

1½ cups all-purpose flour

1 teaspoon baking soda

1 teaspoon ground cinnamon

½ cup (1 stick) unsalted butter, at room temperature

1 cup tightly packed light brown sugar

½ cup granulated sugar

2 large eggs, at room temperature

1 teaspoon pure vanilla extract

3 cups uncooked quick or old-fashioned oats

1 cup dried blueberries

1 cup semisweet chocolate chips, optional

I'm not going to fib—I got this recipe off a box of Quaker Oats years ago, but I've been making these cookies for so long and so frequently that everybody in my house thinks I invented them. I usually add dried blueberries rather than the standard raisins, and often add chocolate bits, too.

Preheat the oven to 350°F.

Combine the flour, baking soda, and cinnamon in a mixing bowl. Set aside.

Place the butter in the bowl of a standing electric mixer fitted with the paddle and beat on medium until softened. Add the brown and granulated sugars and continue to beat on medium until light and creamy. Add the eggs, one at a time, beating well after each addition. Beat in the vanilla.

Add the flour mixture and beat to just blend. Add the oatmeal and beat to incorporate.

Remove the bowl from the mixer and stir in the blueberries and the chocolate chips, if using.

Drop the batter by tablespoonfuls onto ungreased cookie sheets. Bake for about 10 minutes or until cooked through and golden brown around the edges. Using a spatula, transfer the cookies to wire racks to cool.

When cool, store in an airtight container at room temperature.

Note: You can also make the dough into bar cookies by smoothing it into an ungreased (nonstick is great) 9- by 13-inch baking pan. Bake at 350°F for about 30 minutes or until set and golden brown. Cool on a wire rack and then, using a serrated knife, cut into bars or squares when cool.

PEAR-BLUEBERRY **CRISP**

Serves 8 to 10

2½ pounds firm pears, peeled,
cored, and cut into chunks

3 cups blueberries

Grated zest and juice of 1 lemon

⅓ cup plus ½ cup tightly packed
light brown sugar

2 tablespoons cornstarch

1 cup all-purpose flour

¼ cup granulated sugar

1 teaspoon ground nutmeg
or ginger (see Note)

½ cup (1 stick) chilled unsalted
butter, cut into small pieces

½ cup quick oats

½ cup chopped nuts (almonds,
hazelnuts, or pecans)

Whipped cream, vanilla ice cream,
or frozen yogurt for serving

This combination of fruit is one of our favorites, but I make crisps and cobblers from all types of fruit year-round: pears and apples in the winter and soft fruits and berries in the summer. You can combine a mix of fruits or use just one type. This is a simple dessert that my mom made and one that has been made in American kitchens since the early settlers had the barest of ingredients to work with.

Preheat the oven to 375°F. Generously butter the interior of a 3-quart baking dish or skillet.

Combine the pears and blueberries in a large mixing bowl. Add the lemon zest and juice, tossing to coat well. Add the ⅓ cup brown sugar along with the cornstarch and again toss to coat well. Scrape the fruit mixture into the prepared baking dish.

Place the flour in the bowl of a food processor fitted with the metal blade. Add the remaining ½ cup brown sugar along with the granulated sugar and nutmeg and pulse to blend. Add the chilled butter, a bit at a time, processing until crumbly.

Remove the bowl from the mixer and stir in the oats and nuts. Evenly sprinkle the topping over the fruit.

Bake the crisp for about 30 minutes or until the fruit is bubbling and the topping is golden brown and crisp.

Let rest for about 30 minutes before serving. This will give the juicy fruit some time to jell a bit. Serve warm with whipped cream, ice cream, or frozen yogurt.

Note: If you flavor the topping with ground ginger, you might like to add about a tablespoon of grated fresh ginger to the fruit mix. It adds just a hint of spice to the sweetness.

CHAPTER 8

SNACK TIME

A little of this and a little of that—just a few tasty treats that can nip hunger in the bud, accompany a glass of wine or cocktail, or offer a little comfort on a cold afternoon.

EMPANADAS

Makes 1 dozen

½ cup raisins

3 tablespoons olive oil

½ cup minced onion

1 clove garlic, minced

1 teaspoon minced red hot chile

¼ cup toasted pine nuts

¼ cup chopped pimento-stuffed green olives

½ pound ground beef chuck

½ teaspoon red pepper flakes

½ teaspoon ground cumin

Pinch ground cinnamon

Salt and pepper

Short Pastry for Tarts and Pies (page 168)

1 large egg

This is an easy filling to put together, and, believe me, if you don't have time to make the pastry, nobody will know if you use commercially prepared refrigerated piecrusts (such as those from Pillsbury). We keep a supply in the freezer all the time so anyone can have a snack on a few minute's notice. Although the filling is representative of classic Latin American flavors, you can use any protein and seasonings you like: meat, fish, poultry, or even vegetables. If you want smaller empanadas to serve with cocktails, cut the dough into about 2½-inch rounds; this should yield at least 2 dozen hors d'oeuvres. They should be fully baked in about 20 minutes.

Line a baking sheet with a silicone liner or parchment paper.

Place the raisins in a small heat-proof bowl and cover with 1 cup boiling water. Set aside to hydrate for at least 10 minutes.

Heat the oil in a large heavy frying pan over medium heat. Add the onion, garlic, and chile and cook, stirring frequently, for about 10 minutes or until slightly colored. Add the pine nuts and olives and continue to cook, stirring occasionally, for 3 minutes. Add the beef along with the red pepper flakes, cumin, and cinnamon. Season with salt and pepper and cook, stirring occasionally, for about 5 minutes or just until the beef is no longer pink.

Drain the raisins well and stir them into the beef mixture. Set aside to cool slightly.

Roll out each piece of dough to ⅛-inch thickness.

Using a large round cookie cutter (or a bowl), cut out twelve 5-inch rounds from the dough and place on a clean work surface.

Using a tablespoon, mound an equal portion of the cooled beef mixture into the center of each pastry round. Using a pastry brush, lightly coat the edges with just a hint of cool water. Fold the pastry round in half, enclosing the filling and forming a half-moon shape. Gently press the edges together and then crimp them closed with a

fork. As made, transfer the empanadas to the prepared baking sheet. Prick the tops with the tines of the fork to make air vents. (At this point, the empanadas may be frozen on the baking sheet. Once frozen, pack into resealable plastic bags or plastic containers. Egg wash and bake when needed; the baking time for the frozen empanadas will be an additional 7 minutes.)

Preheat the oven to 450°F.

Combine the egg with 1 tablespoon cold water in a small bowl and vigorously whisk to lighten.

Using a pastry brush, lightly coat the top of each empanada with the egg wash. Transfer the baking sheet to the preheated oven and bake for 10 minutes. Lower the heat to 325°F and continue to bake for another 20 minutes or until the empanadas are golden brown.

Let the empanadas rest for 5 minutes before serving hot, or let cool to room temperature and serve. Baked empanadas can also be cooled and then frozen as above. Do not thaw before reheating. Reheat in a 350°F oven for about 15 minutes.

ROASTED **EDAMAME**

Makes about 4 cups

2 pounds frozen edamame,
in the pod

2 tablespoons avocado oil

2 teaspoons toasted sesame oil

1 tablespoon soy sauce

Cracked black pepper

Until recently, we thought of soybeans only as fodder for livestock or for oil, but with the explosion of Asian cooking we have embraced tofu and soy milk, and now edamame: steamed soybeans in the pod that can be found at the beginning of every sushi meal. Since we are sushi lovers, edamame has become one of our favorite Japanese snacks. Rather than steaming, I like to roast them, either in the oven or outdoors in my wood-fired oven, which really gives the finished roast a wonderful smoky flavor. If you can find them, fresh edamame are particularly easy to roast as they don't have the excess moisture of the frozen. Don't eat the pods, just enjoy popping the beans straight into your mouth.

Place the edamame in a colander in the sink (or over a large bowl) and let drain for about 1 hour or until thawed.

Preheat the oven to 375°F.

Transfer the edamame to a double layer of paper towels to drain off any excess water, then pat dry. Place in a large bowl, add the avocado and sesame oils, soy sauce, and pepper and toss to coat well.

Spread the seasoned edamame on a large rimmed baking sheet in an even layer. Roast, turning occasionally, for about 30 minutes or until the pods puff up and the skins are browning. Serve immediately.

MIXED VEGETABLE **CHIPS**

Makes about 10 cups

1 large sweet potato, peeled

1 large Idaho potato, peeled

1 celery root, peeled

1 large beet, peeled

1 large carrot, peeled

Canola oil for deep frying

Salt

I like to keep a batch of these chips on hand for many reasons. They make a terrific light snack; they are the perfect side for sandwiches, burgers, and dogs; and they are addictive with cocktails on the deck or patio. You really can use any vegetable you like, but this combo is one of my favorites.

Using a Japanese vegetable slicer (see Note) and working with one vegetable at a time, cut the vegetables into potato chip–thin slices. As sliced, dry well with paper towels as any moisture will dilute the hot oil and affect the ability of the chips to brown quickly.

Heat the oil in a deep-fat fryer over medium-high heat to 350°F on a candy thermometer.

Place a few vegetable slices at a time in the hot oil so that they don't stick together. Fry for about 1 minute or until lightly colored and crisp. Using either the fryer basket or a slotted spoon, transfer the chips to a double layer of paper towels to drain.

Season with salt and serve at room temperature.

Note: A Japanese mandoline slicer (also known as a Benriner) is an inexpensive tool that cuts vegetables and fruits into slices of varying thickness. It has three different blades that create uniform slices that range from paper-thin to chunky. Indispensable for fine cuts, it usually sells for less than $50.00. The more expensive French mandoline works in the same fashion.

BLACK BEAN MASH

Makes about 5 cups

2 tablespoons bacon fat
or canola oil

1 large onion, chopped

4 cloves garlic, chopped

2 (19-ounce) cans black beans,
well drained

1 cup shredded Jack, pepper Jack,
or cheddar cheese

¼ cup light beer

2 teaspoons ground cumin

½ teaspoon paprika

Hot pepper sauce, such
as Tabasco (to taste)

Salt

3 tablespoons chopped cilantro

Tortilla chips or vegetable
sticks, for serving

This is a great have-on-hand mash. It works both as a dip and as a filling for burritos, enchiladas, or tacos. If you like a little heat, add 1 hot green chile to the beans when you puree them. A bowl of Guacamole (page 103) is a welcome partner.

Heat the bacon fat or oil in a medium frying pan over medium heat. Add the onion and garlic and cook, stirring frequently, for about 5 minutes or just until softened. Remove from the heat.

Combine the drained beans with the cheese, beer, cumin, paprika, and hot sauce in the bowl of a food processor fitted with the metal blade. Scrape the onion mixture into the bowl and process to a smooth, thick puree. Season with salt to taste.

Scrape into a serving bowl or a nonreactive container and stir the cilantro into the mix. If not using immediately, cover and refrigerate for up to 1 week.

Serve at room temperature with tortilla chips or vegetable sticks.

KALE CROSTONE

Serves 6

1 bunch organic *cavalo nero* or other kale, well washed and patted dry

12 (½-inch-thick) slices peasant bread

2 cloves garlic, peeled

Salt and pepper

¼ cup high-quality extra-virgin olive oil, such as from Zamparelli

There is almost nothing more satisfying than this simple dish, as long as the vegetables used are garden-fresh and the olive oil is of spectacular quality. This is the mother of the more familiar crostini, the traditional diminutive Tuscan snack. Although I use kale—the deeply green, almost black *cavalo nero* (also called Tuscan kale, dinosaur kale, and black kale) is the best—you could use almost any leafy vegetable as long as it is very flavorful. This works as a snack because you can cook the kale and hold it in some of its cooking water and make the toast to have on hand. Then you just need a quick warm-up for both, either on the stovetop or in the oven or microwave.

Bring a large pot of salted water to a boil over high heat.

Carefully remove the tough rib from the center of each kale leaf. Drop the kale into the boiling water and cook for 30 minutes or until very tender.

While the kale is cooking, toast the bread. While still warm, lightly rub one side of each piece of toast with the garlic. Season with salt and pepper to taste.

Using tongs, gently lift a small amount of kale from the pot and lay it over the top of the seasoned toast. Don't try to drain the kale; you want the cooking water to flavor the bread. Drizzle a spoonful of the cooking water over the kale and then finish with a drizzle of olive oil and more salt and pepper to taste. Serve warm.

EXTRA-RICH
HOT CHOCOLATE

Serves 6

4 ounces unsweetened chocolate

2 ounces milk chocolate

1 tablespoon unsalted butter

3 ounces heavy cream

¼ cup sugar

6 cups very hot milk

Marshmallows (recipe follows)

There is nothing more welcoming to a houseful of kids than steaming hot chocolate topped with marshmallows and, you know what, adults like it just as well. We always have some ganache on hand so I can heat up a mug for movie watching or an after-game treat. We try to make our own marshmallows or, at the least, purchase some of the great handmade ones. However, we also keep those Campfire favorites on hand, just in case.

Combine the chocolates with the butter in a heat-proof bowl.

Combine the cream and sugar in a medium saucepan over medium-low heat. Bring to a boil and immediately remove from the heat. Beating constantly, pour the hot mixture over the chocolate. When perfectly blended, pour the mixture into a 4- by 6-inch pan and set aside to cool.

When cool, cut the ganache into 1-inch squares. You can store the ganache, tightly covered and refrigerated, for up to 5 days.

Place 2 squares of ganache into each of 6 mugs (for rich hot choco-late). Add a cup of hot milk to each one, stirring to melt the ganache. Place as many marshmallows as you like in each mug and serve.

MARSHMALLOWS

Makes about 24

½ cup confectioners' sugar

¼ cup cornstarch

3½ cups plus 1 tablespoon granulated sugar

1 cup light corn syrup

2 packets granulated gelatin

Set up a standing electric mixer with the whip attachment.

Combine the confectioners' sugar and cornstarch in a baking pan and spread it out in an even layer over the bottom of the pan. Set aside.

Combine the granulated sugar and corn syrup with ¼ cup cool water in a heavy-bottomed saucepan over medium heat. Bring to a simmer and cook, stirring occasionally, for about 12 minutes or until the mixture reaches 116°F on a candy thermometer.

While the syrup is cooking, combine the gelatin with ¼ cup cool water in a small saucepan. Set aside to "bloom" for about 3 minutes. Then place over low heat and heat just until the gelatin has completely melted.

Transfer the gelatin to the mixer bowl. With the motor running on the lowest setting, begin pouring the hot syrup into the gelatin. The syrup will combine with the gelatin and begin to create a meringue-like mixture. Continue beating until the mixture is cool enough to handle and very stiff. (At this point you can flavor the mixture with any spice, vanilla, or liqueur.)

Transfer the marshmallow mixture to a pastry bag fitted with a large, plain round tip. Pipe marshmallow-sized rounds onto the prepared baking pan. When all of the marshmallows are piped, carefully roll each one in the sugar/cornstarch mixture.

Store, tightly covered in layers separated by waxed paper, for up to 2 days.

CRANBERRY-ORANGE BREAD

Makes one 9-inch loaf

2 cups sifted all-purpose flour

¾ cup sugar

1½ teaspoons baking powder

½ teaspoon salt

½ teaspoon baking soda

1 cup coarsely chopped cranberries

½ cup chopped walnuts

1 tablespoon grated orange zest

1 large egg

¾ cup orange juice

2 tablespoons canola oil

This is just one of many fruit breads we keep on hand, and when the boys were much younger we often kept an assortment handy. If not too sweet, fruit breads such as this one (or banana, apricot, lemon, squash, or pumpkin) are great for breakfast, as well as a lunch treat, afternoon nibble, or late-night snack.

Preheat the oven to 350°F. Lightly coat the interior of a 9-inch loaf pan with nonstick cooking spray or butter. If using butter, lightly flour the pan.

Sift the flour, sugar, baking powder, salt, and baking soda together into a large mixing bowl. Add the cranberries, walnuts, and orange zest, stirring to blend.

Combine the egg, orange juice, and oil in a small bowl, whisking to combine. Pour into the flour mixture, stirring until just moistened. Do not overmix.

Scrape the batter into the prepared loaf pan. Bake for about 50 minutes or until a cake tester inserted into the center comes out clean and the bread is golden brown.

Invert the pan onto a wire rack. Remove the pan, turn the bread right side up, and let cool. Do not slice until the bread has cooled a bit or it will crumble.

CHAPTER 9

DELICIOUS **DESSERTS**

In our house desserts are not an every-night thing. At most, when a sweet is called for during the week, a store-bought gelato or sorbet might make it to the table. But on weekends and special occasions, I am the dessert king. In the early days of my flagship restaurant Aureole, we were known for our towering, ornate desserts. In fact, diners often came just for the excitement at the end of the meal. You won't find me creating these extravaganzas at home, but I still like to bake and create desserts that everyone can enjoy, even simple ones.

DOUBLE-TROUBLE
CHOCOLATE CHIP COOKIES

Makes about 3 dozen

4 ounces unsweetened chocolate

1¼ cups plus 2 tablespoons
(2¾ sticks) unsalted butter,
at room temperature

1½ cups granulated sugar

½ cup tightly packed
light brown sugar

2 large eggs, at room temperature

1 tablespoon pure vanilla extract

3 cups all-purpose flour

3 tablespoons Dutch-processed
cocoa powder

12 ounces white chocolate chips

1½ cups chopped dry-roasted
salted peanuts

Where's the double trouble? It's those white chocolate chips and salty peanuts nestled into a rich chocolate dough that make these cookies irresistible and double trouble for those with a sweet tooth. If you want to triple your trouble, cut the white chocolate chips to 6 ounces and add 6 ounces of bittersweet chocolate chips to the mix.

Preheat the oven to 325°F. Line 2 baking sheets with nonstick silicone liners or parchment paper.

Place the unsweetened chocolate in a microwavable container. Place in the microwave and heat to melt following the microwave manufacturer's directions, usually at about 50 percent for a minute. Remove from the microwave and stir to blend completely. If the chocolate has not melted completely, return to the microwave and process for a few more seconds. If you don't have a microwave, place the chocolate in a heat-proof bowl set over a small saucepan of boiling water and stir until the chocolate melts. Do not allow the bottom of the bowl to touch the boiling water or the chocolate will cook rather than melt. Remove the bowl from the saucepan, but keep warm.

Place the butter in the bowl of a standing electric mixer fitted with the paddle attachment. Beat on low to just soften, then raise the speed to medium and add the granulated sugar and beat for about 4 minutes or until blended. Add the brown sugar and again beat for another 4 to 5 minutes or until creamy. Add the eggs, one at a time, beating until incorporated. Add the reserved melted chocolate along with the vanilla and beat to blend.

Combine the flour and cocoa powder. Lower the speed of the mixer and begin adding the flour mixture, a bit at a time, scraping down the sides of the bowl as you add. Continue adding flour and beating until the mixture is smooth and well-blended.

Continued

Remove the bowl from the mixer and, using a wooden spoon, beat in the white chocolate chips and peanuts.

Spoon about 2 tablespoons cookie dough into your hands. Form into a ball and place on a prepared baking sheet. Repeat to make about 36 balls, placing them about 3 inches apart on the sheets.

Bake the cookies for about 15 minutes or until the cookies are barely brown around the edges and set in the middle.

Let rest for about 2 minutes. Using a spatula, transfer the cookies to wire racks to cool.

Store, covered in a cool spot, for up to 3 days.

LEMON **SHORTBREAD**

Makes about 32 small wedges or 8 dozen small cookies

1 pound (4 sticks) unsalted
butter, at room temperature

1 cup sugar

Zest and juice of 1 large
organic lemon

4⅓ to 5 cups sifted
all-purpose flour

Sanding sugar or candy
sprinkles, optional

Shortbread cookies are traditionally cut into wedges, but they are very, very simple cookies that turn into little gems when you use a cookie press to form flowers, butterflies, wreaths, or whatever disk you choose. They freeze extremely well, either unbaked or baked, so they can easily be baked, or thawed and warmed, for last-minute treats or dessert. Shortbread is a great garnish for ice cream sundaes, puddings, and fruit desserts.

Combine the butter and sugar in the bowl of a heavy-duty electric mixer fitted with the paddle. Beat on low to blend; then add the lemon juice, raise the speed to medium, and beat for about 4 minutes or until very light.

Slowly add the flour, beating until a soft, firm dough forms, scraping down the sides of the bowl from time to time. Depending upon the weather, the lemon juice, and the moisture in your butter, you may not need all of the flour.

Remove the bowl from the mixer and, using a wooden spoon, beat the lemon zest into the dough. (If you do this with the mixer, the zest tends to stick to the paddle.)

When blended, cover the dough and refrigerate for about 30 minutes to firm up a bit.

Preheat the oven to 300°F. If baking the shortbread in pans, set out two 9-inch round pie or cake pans. If using a cookie press to form cookies, line 2 baking sheets with nonstick silicone liners or parchment paper.

To bake the shortbread in pans, divide the dough into 2 equal pieces. Working with one piece at a time, pack the dough into the cake or pie pan, pressing it into a flat circle. Using a table fork, prick the entire top. If desired, sprinkle sanding sugar or candy sprinkles over the top. Bake the cookies for about 30 minutes, frequently checking to make sure the

cookies are not browning too quickly. They should be a very pale gold when done. Remove from the oven and immediately cut into small wedges, then let cool in the pan.

If using a cookie press, set it up with whatever die you are going to use. Remove the dough from the refrigerator and fill the cookie press. Press cookies directly onto the prepared cookie sheets, leaving about 1½ inches between them. If desired, sprinkle the tops with sanding sugar or candy sprinkles. Bake the cookies for about 18 minutes, frequently checking to make sure the cookies are not browning too quickly. They should be a very pale gold when done. Remove from the oven and transfer to wire racks to cool.

PRALINE BARS

Makes about 3 dozen

½ cup (1 stick) unsalted butter, at room temperature

1½ cups tightly packed dark brown sugar

1 large egg, at room temperature

1 teaspoon pure vanilla extract

1½ cups sifted all-purpose flour

1½ cups chopped pecans

These have always been a kids' favorite in our house. But really, who doesn't like praline? The bars are toffee-like and quite rich in flavor. For an extra kick, sprinkle the dough with butterscotch chips and let them melt into the bars as they bake.

Preheat the oven to 325°F. Lightly spray the interior of an 8-inch square baking pan with nonstick cooking spray.

Combine the butter and sugar in the bowl of a heavy-duty electric mixer fitted with the paddle. Beat on low to blend, then raise the speed to medium and beat for about 4 minutes or until very light. Beat in the egg and vanilla.

Slowly add the flour and beat, scraping down the sides of the bowl from time to time, until completely blended.

Remove the bowl from the mixer and, using a wooden spoon, beat in the pecans. (If you do this with the mixer, the nuts will pulverize.)

Scrape the dough into the prepared pan and smooth the top with a spatula. Bake for about 25 minutes or until golden brown and set. Place on a wire rack to cool.

When cool, cut into squares. Store, tightly covered in layers, at room temperature for up to 1 week.

SO-EASY-RANDALL-CAN-MAKE-IT
CHOCOLATE CAKE

Makes one 8-inch cake

¾ cup Dutch-processed cocoa powder, plus more for dusting

¾ cup all-purpose flour

½ teaspoon baking powder

1½ cups tightly packed dark brown sugar

¾ cup buttermilk

⅓ cup canola oil

1 teaspoon pure almond extract

Confectioners' sugar for dusting

This is a spectacularly good chocolate cake that is easy as pie to put together. I always like to keep a chocolate dessert in the house, and this one is such a favorite even our non-cook, Randall, can make it. It makes a light snack, but with a bit of ice cream, frozen yogurt, mascarpone cheese, or crème fraîche, you quickly have an almost-fancy end of the meal.

Preheat the oven to 325°F. Generously coat the interior of an 8-inch square baking dish with butter. Lightly dust with cocoa powder, taking care that the entire pan is coated with a fine layer.

Sift the cocoa, flour, and baking powder together into a mixing bowl. When blended, stir in the brown sugar, mixing to blend completely.

Combine the buttermilk, oil, and extract in a large measuring cup until blended. Slowly pour into the dry ingredients, beating until smooth.

Pour the batter into the prepared pan and smooth down the top with a spatula. Bake for about 40 minutes or until a cake tester inserted into the center comes out clean. Place on a wire rack to cool.

When cool, combine a bit of cocoa powder and confectioners' sugar in a fine mesh sieve placed over the cooled cake. Tap gently on the edge of the sieve to lightly dust the cake.

When ready to serve, cut into squares. May be stored, tightly covered in a cool spot, for up to 3 days.

Wine Pairing: Rockpile Independence Red Wine (port wine) from Clay Mauritson, which is one of the only true port wines produced in all of California.

HAZELNUT
POUND CAKE

Makes one 10-inch round cake

---

1 pound (4 sticks) unsalted butter,
at room temperature

1¾ cups sugar

1 tablespoon pure vanilla extract

10 large eggs, at
room temperature

4 cups sifted cake flour

2 cups finely chopped hazelnuts

2 teaspoons grated orange zest

I always laugh when someone tells me that a dessert is a "good keeper," knowing full well that desserts never last long enough in our house to keep. That said, there is nothing that keeps as well as a buttery pound cake. At room temperature, well wrapped, it will keep for a week, and for up to 3 months in the freezer. Thaw and warm before serving, and it will taste like it just came out of the oven.

Preheat the oven to 325°F. Lightly coat the interior of a Bundt pan with nonstick cooking spray.

Place the butter in the bowl of a heavy-duty electric mixer fitted with the paddle. Beat on low until light and creamy. Raise the speed to medium, add the sugar and vanilla, and beat for about 4 minutes or until very light and fluffy.

Add the eggs, one at a time, beating well and scraping down the sides of the bowl after each addition. Slowly add the flour and beat, scraping down the sides of the bowl from time to time, until completely blended.

Remove the bowl from the mixer and, using a wooden spoon, beat in the hazelnuts and orange zest.

Scrape the mixture into the prepared Bundt pan and lightly smooth the top with a spatula. Bake for about 1 hour or until a cake tester inserted into the center comes out clean.

Invert the pan onto a wire rack. Lift off the pan and let the cake cool.

When cool, store in a cool spot, covered tightly, for up to 1 week.

PEAR TARTE TATIN

Makes one 9-inch tart

¾ cup tightly packed
light brown sugar

½ cup (1 stick) unsalted butter,
at room temperature

5 large firm pears, peeled, cored,
and cut into quarters

1 piece frozen puff pastry
(see Note), thawed

Whipped cream, crème fraîche,
frozen vanilla yogurt, or caramel ice
cream, for serving, optional

Although the classic French tarte tatin is usually made with sweet apples, I actually prefer crisp pears as they aren't quite as sweet, yet caramelize in the same way. Frozen puff pastry makes this a snap to put together. Using a nonstick, ovenproof frying pan makes unmolding the tart incredibly easy as well: No sticking and no mess, and the pears will unmold in a perfect pattern.

Preheat the oven to 375°F.

Combine the sugar and ¼ cup cold water in an 8-inch nonstick, ovenproof frying pan over low heat. Cook, stirring constantly, for about 3 minutes or until the sugar has dissolved. Raise the heat to medium and bring to a boil. Allow to cook at a gentle boil, without stirring, for about 6 minutes or until a golden syrup has formed. Stir in the butter and cook, stirring, until well blended.

Remove the pan from the heat and carefully arrange the pear quarters, cut sides facing up, in a slightly overlapping circle in the caramel, and place 2 or 3 halves in the middle to fill any open space.

Lightly flour a clean, flat work surface. Place the pastry on the floured surface and, using a rolling pin, roll the pastry out to a shape large enough to cut out a circle about 9 inches in diameter. Using a pastry wheel or paring knife, cut out the circle and place over the pears. Fold the excess edge under to enclose the fruit. Using a paring knife, cut at least 4 slits in the center of the pastry to allow steam to escape.

Bake the tart for about 35 minutes or until the pastry has puffed and is golden brown.

Let cool on a wire rack for about 5 minutes to set. Using a small sharp knife, loosen the edges from the pan and then place the serving platter over the pan and carefully invert the tart onto it. Remove the pan.

Serve warm, with a topping of choice if you like.

Note: Both Trader Joe's and Dufour make excellent frozen puff pastry. The first is, obviously, available at Trader Joe's markets; Dufour is available at many supermarkets and specialty food stores as well as online.

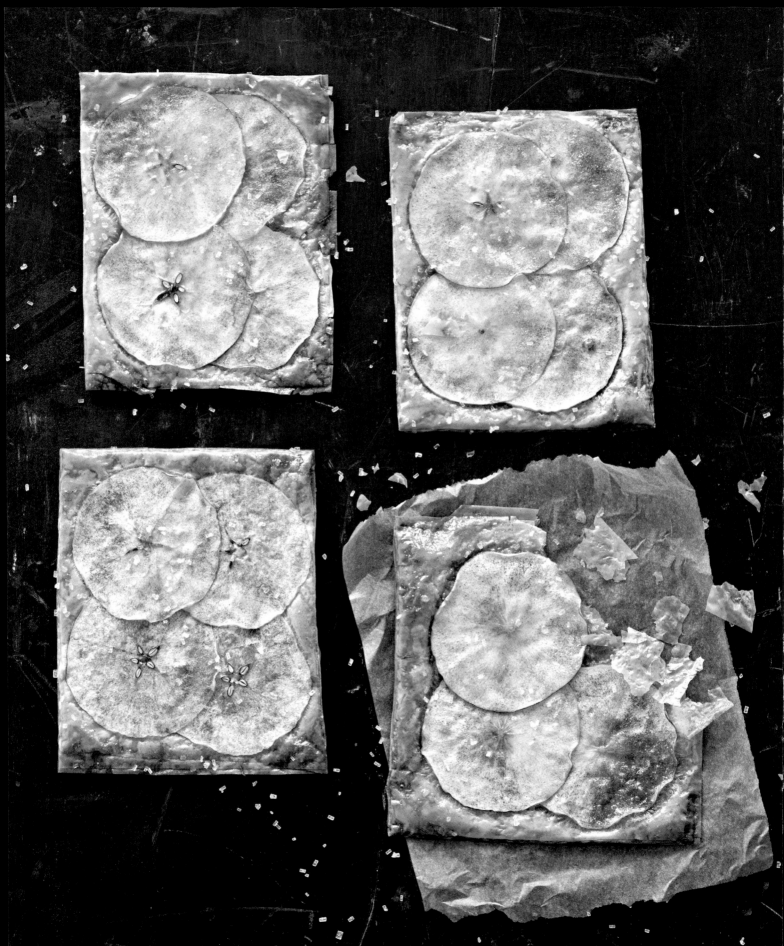

HANDHELD
APPLE TARTS

Serves 6

1 large organic apple

6 sheets phyllo (filo) pastry

¼ cup (½ stick) unsalted
butter, melted

3 tablespoons boiled cider,
apple, or pure maple syrup

½ teaspoon ground cinnamon

About 2 tablespoons white
sanding sugar

Cinnamon or vanilla ice cream,
for serving, optional

I call these handheld tarts because they are so easy to pick up and eat, but there is no reason you can't bring them to the table on a plate, particularly if you garnish them with a scoop of ice cream. I like the rich flavor of the boiled cider syrup, but if you can't find it, apple syrup or maple syrup will do just fine.

Preheat the oven to 350°F. Line a baking sheet with a nonstick silicone liner or parchment paper.

Peel the apple and, using a sharp knife, trim off each end. Using a Japanese mandoline slicer (see Note on page 211), cut the apple into paper-thin slices. Wrap the apple slices in a damp paper towel and set aside.

Remove the 6 sheets of phyllo dough from the package and immediately cover them with a damp kitchen towel.

Combine the melted butter with the syrup and cinnamon, stirring to blend completely.

Working with one sheet of the phyllo at a time while keeping the remaining sheets covered, use a pastry brush to generously coat one piece of pastry with the melted butter mixture. Top with another sheet and continue to butter and stack until all of the pastry sheets have been used.

Using a pizza cutter, cut the stacked dough into 6 equal pieces. Transfer the pastry pieces to the prepared baking sheet.

Unwrap the apple slices and lightly coat 16 to 20 slices with the remaining butter mixture. Working with one at a time, carefully place 4 or 5 apple slices, buttered side up, in a single layer on top of each piece of pastry. The number of slices required will depend upon the size of your apple; if large enough, 4 slices should do it. Sprinkle the top of each tart with sanding sugar.

Bake the tarts for about 12 minutes or until the pastry is golden brown and the apple slices are slightly turned on the edges and touched with color.

Serve hot, with a scoop of ice cream, if desired.

FIG CROSTATA

Makes one 9-inch tart

¼ cup all-purpose flour, sifted

2 cups whole milk

3 large eggs, at room temperature

5 tablespoons sugar

1 teaspoon pure vanilla extract

8 whole fresh figs

Tart Pastry Shell (recipe follows)

2 tablespoons Marsala wine, rum, or bourbon

¼ cup tightly packed light brown sugar

I first had a taste of a fruit crostata in Tuscany, where dessert is usually just a fig or other fruit and some cheese. A crostata rather mimics a French tart but is a bit more rustic in appearance. We have more figs than we know what to do with in Sonoma, so this tart is frequently found on our table in the fall.

Preheat the oven to 350°F.

Whisk the flour into the milk in a medium, heavy-bottomed saucepan. When well-blended, whisk in the eggs until incorporated. Whisk in the sugar and vanilla. Place over medium heat and cook, stirring constantly, for about 5 minutes or until the mixture comes to a boil. Lower the heat and cook at a low simmer, stirring constantly, for 3 minutes. Immediately remove from the heat and allow to cool slightly.

Cut the figs lengthwise in half. Pour the slightly cooled cream into the tart shell and immediately lay the figs, cut side up, over the filling. They should cover the entire top of the tart. Sprinkle the wine or liquor over the top and then lightly dust with the brown sugar.

Bake for 40 minutes or until the cream has set and the figs are lightly browned.

Place on a wire rack to cool slightly before cutting.

2½ cups all-purpose
flour, sifted

1 cup minus 1 tablespoon sugar

2 tablespoons baking powder

2 large eggs, at room temperature

7 tablespoons unsalted butter,
at room temperature

TART PASTRY SHELL

Makes enough for one 9-inch tart

This pastry can be used for any number of sweet or savory pies or tarts. However, when making a savory tart, you should eliminate the entire amount of sugar.

Line the bottom of a 9-inch tart pan with a piece of parchment paper cut to fit.

Combine the flour, sugar, and baking powder in a large mixing bowl. Add the eggs and butter and, using your hands, lightly knead the mixture together until it is of a fairly uniform texture. Don't overmix or the dough will be tough.

Transfer the dough to the prepared tart pan and, using your fingertips, begin gently spreading the dough into the pan until it covers the bottom and sides evenly.

The tart shell may be made in advance and stored, covered and refrigerated, for 1 day, or frozen for up to 3 months. Thaw before using.

CHILLED ORANGE
SOUFFLÉ

Serves 6

1 tablespoon cornstarch

1 cup heavy cream

1 tablespoon unflavored gelatin

4 large eggs, separated

½ cup superfine sugar

½ cup Cointreau

2 teaspoons freshly grated orange zest

½ teaspoon cream of tartar

Whipped cream for garnish, optional

When cooking at home I am a big proponent of make-ahead desserts. It just seems easier to know that dessert is done before I start organizing my main course. I think it is good advice for all home cooks to follow. Chilled soufflés fit the bill: make-ahead, elegant, refreshing, and a welcome end to the meal.

You can also make individual soufflés in 6-ounce ramekins following the same instructions as for the large one.

Lightly coat the interior of six 6-ounce soufflé dishes or a 1½-quart soufflé mold with nonstick cooking spray. Measure a double piece of waxed paper to fit around the outside of each dish and come 1 inch above the rim. Either tape it in place or tie it closed with kitchen twine. Lightly coat the interior of the paper rim with nonstick cooking spray. Set the mold aside.

Combine the cornstarch with 2 tablespoons cool water in a medium saucepan, whisking to blend well. Add the cream and place over low heat. Cook, stirring constantly with a wooden spoon, for about 5 minutes or until thickened. Remove from the heat and set aside.

Place ¼ cup cool water in a small bowl. Sprinkle the gelatin on top and stir to combine. Set aside to soften.

Combine the egg yolks with the sugar in the bowl of a standing electric mixer. Place the bowl (not the mixer) over a bowl of hot water; do not allow the bottom of the bowl to touch the water or the eggs will begin to cook. Using a wire whisk, beat the yolk mixture until slightly warm. Transfer the bowl to the mixer stand with the wire whisk attachment and begin beating on low. Gradually raise the speed and beat, occasionally scraping down the sides of the bowl with a rubber spatula, until the mixture is pale yellow and able to form a ribbon when the spatula is pulled through.

Whisk the yolk mixture and the gelatin into the reserved thickened cream mixture. Place over low heat and cook, stirring constantly, for 5 minutes. Remove from the heat and stir in the Cointreau and orange zest.

Continued

Place the egg whites in a clean, dry bowl of the standing mixer. Add the cream of tartar and begin beating on low. Gradually raise the speed to medium-high and beat until firm peaks form. Carefully fold the beaten egg whites into the soufflé base, folding with a rubber spatula to blend without deflating the mixture.

Pour the soufflé mixture into the prepared dishes or mold and smooth down the top with a rubber spatula. Refrigerate for at least 8 hours or until set and well chilled.

When ready to serve, untie the collar and dip each dish or the mold into hot water for about 5 seconds to loosen the soufflé. Invert a chilled serving plate over the top of each dish or the mold and then turn over to unmold the soufflé onto serving plates. Garnish with whipped cream if you like and serve.

CHOCOLATE **PUDDING**

Serves 6

½ cup sugar

⅓ cup cornstarch

¼ cup Dutch-processed cocoa powder

2 cups whole milk

1 teaspoon pure vanilla extract

4 ounces bittersweet chocolate, cut into small pieces

1 tablespoon unsalted butter, at room temperature

Once you take the time to make plain old chocolate pudding, you will never again buy a box of instant. Since it is such an easy dessert and one that kids really do love, it has, over the years, become my quick fix for sweet time. Add a dollop of whipped cream and some chocolate sprinkles or curls, and plain will easily become fancy for a dinner party.

Combine the sugar, cornstarch, and cocoa powder in a heavy-bottomed saucepan. Whisk in the milk and vanilla and place over medium heat. Cook, whisking constantly, for about 6 minutes or until smooth and thick. Add the chocolate and lower the heat. Cook, beating constantly with a wooden spoon, until the pudding is smooth and creamy. Beat in the butter and remove from the heat.

Spoon the pudding into individual dishes or one large bowl. Cover with plastic wrap (do not allow the wrap to touch the pudding) and set aside to cool before serving. May be stored, covered and refrigerated, for up to 2 days.

FRESH FRUIT
GRANITAS

Makes about 4½ cups, or enough to serve 6 people

4 cups thawed frozen strawberries, raspberries, or blueberries; OR
4 cups watermelon juice; OR
4 cups strained fresh orange, grapefruit, blood orange, tangerine, or lemon juice

½ cup Sugar Syrup (recipe follows)

There is nothing more refreshing than a fruit granita at the end of a meal, or on a hot summer's afternoon lazing on a hammock or stretched out on the deck. You can use this recipe for any fruit or vegetable juice. I have made beet, cucumber, and carrot granitas to serve with shellfish—an unexpected twist, but one that absolutely works.

To make berry juice, combine the thawed berries with 4 cups cold water in a medium saucepan over medium heat. Bring to a simmer and immediately remove from the heat. Strain through a fine mesh sieve. Measure out 4 cups of the berry liquid and set it aside to cool.

For the berry juice and all other juices, combine the 4 cups juice with the syrup and pour into a shallow container. An old-fashioned metal ice cube tray is perfect; a shallow plastic container will also work.

Place in the freezer and freeze for at least 3 hours or until very hard.

When ready to serve, remove the granita from the freezer. Using a table fork, scrape back and forth over the top, pulling the frozen ice into thin shards.

Place in small glasses and serve immediately.

1 cup sugar

SUGAR SYRUP

Makes about 1½ cups

Combine the sugar with 1 cup cold water in a small heavy saucepan over medium heat. Bring to a simmer and simmer for about 3 minutes or until the sugar has completely dissolved. Remove from the heat and let cool.

Store, covered and refrigerated, for up to 1 month.

Sugar syrup is a great boon for dessert and drink making. It is usually made with equal parts sugar and water, but it you want a thicker syrup, you can up the sugar to 1¼ parts to 1 part water. That is, 1¼ cups sugar to 1 cup water. I always have it on hand to sweeten iced teas, fruit drinks, and, of course, summertime cocktails.

ACKNOWLEDGMENTS

First and foremost, thank you to my family for their never-ending support and understanding, as well as all of the time spent around the table that provided so much material for this book. Lisa, Courtland, Randall, Reed, and Eric—here's to much more time in the kitchen together and many more suppers around our table.

I'd also like to thank:

Judie, for your dedication and for bringing our family table to life through these pages.

Robyn, Bill, and Melanie, for the brilliant photography.

Karen, for believing in the book and making it all happen.

Christa, Kristyn, and Meredith for putting all the pieces together.

My chefs, managers, and restaurant staff, for their hard work, inspiration, and keeping me on my toes every day.

SOURCES

BEANS
Rancho Gordo
707-259-1935
ranchogordo.com

BEER
Brewery Ommegang
800-544-1809
ommegang.com

BREAD/FLOUR
Amy's Bread
212-462-2038
amysbread.com

King Arthur Flour
800-827-6836
kingarthurflour.com

Sullivan Street Bakery
212-265-5580
sullivanstreetbakery.com

Wildflower Bread Company
888-904-9453
wildflowerbread.com

CHEESE
Bellwether Farms
707-478-8067
bellwetherfarms.com

Di Palo's Fine Foods
212-226-1033
dipaloselects.com

**Point Reyes Farmstead
Cheese Company**
800-591-6878
pointreyescheese.com

Vella Cheese Company
800-848-0505
vellacheese.com

DUCK
Crescent Duck Farms
631-722-8000
crescentduck.com

FISH/SHELLFISH
Hog Island Oyster Co.
415-663-9218
hogislandoysters.com

Lobster Place
212-255-5672
lobsterplace.com

Swan Oyster Depot
415-673-1101
SFSwanoysterdepot.com

HONEY
Bear Foot Honey Farm
707-570-2899
bearfoothoney.com

Bloomfield Bees
707-836-7278
bloomfieldbeeshoney.com

Brooklyn Grange
347-670-3660
brooklyngrangefarm.com

Lavender Bee Farm
707-789-0554
lavenderbeefarm.com

KITCHEN SUPPLIES
AND SPECIALTY FOODS

Eataly
212-229-2560
eataly.com

Sur La Table
800-243-0852
surlatable.com

Williams-Sonoma
877-812-6235
williams-sonoma.com

Zabar's
800-697-6301
zabars.com

Zingerman's
888-636-8162
zingermans.com

MEAT
Black Pig Meat Co.
707-523-4814
blackpigmeatco.com

Flying Pigs Farm
518- 854-3844
flyingpigsfarm.com

Marin Sun Farms
415-663-8997
marinsunfarms.com

OLIVE OIL
Dry Creek Olive Company
707-431-7200
trattorefarms.com

SPANISH PRODUCTS
Despaña Brand Foods
888-779-8617
despanabrandfoods.com

La Tienda
888-331-4362
tienda.com

The Spanish Table
415-388-5043
spanishtable.com

INDEX

ABOUT THE AUTHOR

Charlie Palmer, chef, hotelier, hospitality entrepreneur

Since the beginning of his celebrated career, master chef and hospitality entrepreneur Charlie Palmer has received critical acclaim for his signature Progressive American cooking. Palmer's upbringing in a farm town in upstate New York, along with his education in various kitchens in France and at the Culinary Institute of America, provided him with the inspiration to open Aureole in 1988. Now, more than twenty-five years after Aureole first opened its doors, Palmer helms dozens of notable restaurants and a growing collection of award-winning boutique hotels.

A member of the James Beard Foundation's "Who's Who of Food and Beverage in America," inducted into the casino community's Gaming Hall of Fame in 2011, and named chairman of the board of trustees of the Culinary Institute of America in 2012, Palmer is a respected and admired figure in American hospitality. A frequent guest on NBC's *Today*, Charlie Palmer is also the author of five cookbooks, including *Great American Food* and *Charlie Palmer's Practical Guide to the New American Kitchen*. He lives in New York City and Healdsburg, California.